AGENCIES WORKING TOGETHER

WITHDRAWN

SAGE HUMAN SERVICES GUIDES, VOLUME 28

SAGE HUMAN SERVICES GUIDES

a series of books edited by ARMAND LAUFFER and published in cooperation with the University of Michigan School of Social Work.

AGENCIES WORKING TOGETHER

A Guide to Coordination and Planning

Robert J. ROSSI
Kevin J. GILMARTIN
Charles W. DAYTON

Jurgen WOLFF, *Illustrator*

*Published in cooperation with the University of Michigan
School of Social Work*

SAGE PUBLICATIONS
Beverly Hills / London / New Delhi

For information address:

SAGE Publications, Inc.
275 South Beverly Drive
Beverly Hills, California 90212

SAGE Publications India Pvt. Ltd.
C-236 Defence Colony
New Delhi 110 024, India

SAGE Publications Ltd
28 Banner Street
London EC1Y 8QE, England

Printed in the United States of America

Library of Congress Cataloging in Publication Data

Rossi, Robert J.
   Agencies working together.

   (Sage human services guides ; 28)
   "Published in cooperation with the
University of Michigan School of Social Work."
   Bibliography: p.
   1. Social work administration—United States.
2. Manpower policy—United States.
3. Administrative agencies—United States.
I. Gilmartin, Kevin J. II. Dayton, Charles W.
III. University of Michigan. School of Social
Work. IV. Title. V. Series: Sage human services
guides ; v. 28.
HV91.R72 1982   361'.0068   82-10558
ISBN 0-8039-0973-X

FIRST PRINTING

This guide is a product of an evaluation of local cooperative planning processes
among employment and training agencies pursuant to a contract with the Employment Development Department, State of California (Grant No. 8100-4797). Organizations undertaking such projects under government sponsorship are encouraged to
state their findings and express their judgments freely. Therefore, points of view or
opinions stated in this book do not necessarily represent the official position or
policy of EDD.

CONTENTS

PREFACE

For the three-year period from 1979 to 1982, the State of California sponsored efforts in three counties to improve coordination among the agencies supplying employment, training, and other services. These efforts revealed a wealth of information on this topic in the form of both personal experiences and documentation of past efforts elsewhere. Building on this information, this guide attempts to describe succinctly the various approaches to interagency coordination that have been successfully tried and shows how to go about pursuing them. It describes typical problems encountered in such efforts and offers suggestions for avoiding or solving them. Its intended readers are those working in local agencies such as the following:

- employment training agencies
- rehabilitation agencies
- employment services offices
- vocational education programs at high schools, colleges, regional occupational programs or centers, adult schools, and private vocational schools
- health and mental health agencies
- corrections agencies
- economic development agencies
- child and family services and agencies on aging
- welfare agencies
- community-based organizations, community action agencies, and chambers of commerce.

Should others find it of interest, such as those working in other types of agencies, administrators at the regional or state levels, or representatives of the private sector, so much the better.

Many persons assisted us in the preparation of this guide, either directly or indirectly. Marilynn Slotterbeck, as project officer for the California State CETA Office, was consistently supportive of our decisions concerning style and content, and she helped get us the necessary clearance to publish the book. Pat Bryant of the Employment Development Department, Allan Holmes of the State Department of Education, and Joe Klier of the Department of Rehabilitation served above and beyond the call of duty while on the state's subcommittee overseeing the guide's production. They carefully reviewed every word of the manuscript and suggested many improvements. Bob Little of the Employment Development Department worked closely with the cooperative planning demonstration program from its inception, and we are not the only ones who owe him a debt of gratitude. Many dozens of others reviewed the manuscript at various stages: the State Project Advisory Committee; the project directors, staff, and steering committee members in the three demonstration counties; and other administrators and staff in both state and local agencies. Pat Spurr typed and repeatedly revised the text. Dick Carter then took on the tasks of getting permission from the U.S. Department of Labor for publication and promoting the manuscript until the right publisher was found. To all of you, our sincere thanks.

Robert J. Rossi
Kevin J. Gilmartin
Charles W. Dayton
American Institutes for Research
Palo Alto, California

Chapter 1

AN INTRODUCTION TO
INTERAGENCY COORDINATION

WHAT IS INTERAGENCY COORDINATION?

There are many correct answers to this question. It can be a teacher in a regional vocational training program sending a student to a junior college placement office for help in finding a job related to her training. It can be staff from a vocational rehabilitation agency and an employment training agency consulting on how best to help a youth with learning difficulties find a meaningful job. It can be an employment services office and a child and family services agency conducting a joint assessment of the needs of youth in their community. There can be as many examples of coordinated effort as there are combinations of local education, health, and social service agencies. *What they all have in common is people from two or more agencies working together to improve services to clients.*

While there are clear advantages to agencies working together in such ways, in fact this does not happen very often. Typically, each agency operates under a separate and distinct legal mandate and funding source, with its own administrative structure, geographical boundaries, and specific objectives. Occasionally efforts are made by two or more such agencies to coordinate their services voluntarily, but these efforts tend to be haphazard and unrewarded by the administrative structures of the individual agencies. When these efforts are mandated by their parent agencies at federal and state levels, the results for local-level agencies are typically no more successful or long-lasting. In fact, coordination efforts that are mandated can frustrate all the parties involved if incentives and waivers of individual agency requirements fail to accompany the top-down pronouncements. The result from lack of coordination is often expensive inefficiency for the agencies and confusing gaps or overlaps in services for their clients.

Yet there are many ways in which agencies working in related areas can coordinate with one another without undue expense or difficulty, to their clients' and their own benefit. Some of these approaches, such as establishing networks of cross-referrals, are common already and are quite easy (although there is usually much room for improvement). Others, such as joint program evaluation, are both rare and relatively difficult. Most approaches fall somewhere in between; they range from methods to establish ties with other agencies and set out common objectives to techniques useful in meeting immediate client needs (such as case consultation, joint intake and assessment, and colocation) to joint gathering and use of information and joint program operation. What they require in common is an openness to working with other agencies and the persistence to make interagency coordination work.

An Example of Interagency Coordination

When an employment training agency began its summer youth program in one county, it wanted to let youth who met the age and family income requirements know of the program. A sizable number of such youth were living in families receiving Aid to Families with Dependent Children (AFDC). Thus, in the early spring, the welfare department pulled out its lists of AFDC families that had age-eligible youth. A staff member from the training agency then drafted a letter to these youth, telling them of the summer employment program and inviting them to apply. These letters were addressed using welfare address lists. The result was a higher participation rate in the summer youth program than expected among the intended target group.

As you proceed, you may find yourself unfamiliar with some of the terms used to refer to various cooperative approaches (What is a client conference? A staff loan? An information clearinghouse?). These terms and many others are defined in a *glossary* located at the end of this guide. Refer to this glossary if you are unsure of a term; even those you know may be used slightly differently here from your customary way, and we want to make our use of them clear.

THE BENEFITS OF INTERAGENCY
COORDINATION

A quite sensible question may be occurring to you as you read this chapter: *Why* coordinate with other agencies? Things may be going perfectly well as they are. Why rock the boat? Why invite trouble? There may be no good reason, especially if you:

- have trouble filling your day with useful tasks because so few problems come to your door;
- are already the most effective agency administrator in your part of the state;
- aren't really much interested in your agency's public image;

and your agency:

- has more money than it knows what to do with;
- is already serving every potential client in its bailiwick;
- is providing clients with all the services that they could possibly need;
- makes obtaining its services ridiculously simple; and
- sets efficiency records almost daily, to the point where so many services are provided to so many clients at so little cost that you're in danger of doing everything for everyone for nothing.

Does this sound like your agency? If so, close the book and go relax somewhere. You deserve a rest!

Now, for those of you still with us, was there something in that list that caught your eye? It seems there are some very real benefits to interagency coordination that have been corroborated in study after study. Here they are again listed in slightly different form:

- *Improved staff effectiveness.* Interagency coordination can open up a vast new complement of resources to the innovative administrator. New staff skills, new knowledge, new equipment and facilities, new services—all these may well be available to your clients at other organizations and agencies and are there waiting to be explored.

- *Improved public image.* It probably comes as no surprise that most people like hearing about cooperation between agencies, like hearing about improved efficiency and reduced duplication of efforts, like hearing about cutting through bureaucratic red tape for the benefit of needy clients, and like administrators who take responsibility for initiating such changes.

- *Improved accessibility for clients.* Not only will your clients learn more about services in other agencies, their clients will learn more about your services.

- *Reduced fragmentation of services.* Clients with multiple needs are often on their own in learning about and wading through the bureaucracies of each agency that can help them. Interagency coordination eases this difficulty so that a client is treated as a whole person, not a collection of unrelated problems.

- *Greater efficiency.* Interagency coordination can help an agency to deliver more services for the same money, or the same services for less money, through economies of scale, reduction of duplication, and improved cost-benefit ratios.

Reduced Fragmentation of Services

The relationship between an employment training agency and a rehabilitation agency in one county provides a good example of reduced fragmentation of services. Both agencies are intake points for needy clients, but often a client coming to one needs services best provided by the other. For example, the training agency operates a prevocational class through the local community college. Youth with disabilities are routinely referred to this class by rehabilitation counselors, and they see to it that the equipment, fees, and books for subsequent vocational training are made available through the rehabilitation office. Should a client come to the training agency first and have a disability (whether physical, mental, or emotional), the process works the other way, with the staff there arranging for appropriate services and then sending the client to a rehabilitation counselor to work out the available help from that quarter.

So the advantages are real and meaningful, both to clients and to agencies. This is not to pretend there are no difficulties associated with interagency coordination; there are plenty, and these will be discussed in Chapter 2, along with suggestions for meeting them. There is a growing body of believers, however, who are firmly voicing their commitment to interagency coordination, particularly given the budget cuts many agencies are having to live with and the pressing needs of their clients. As one agency director put it, "It's the only way to maintain any reasonable level of service for our clients with the budget cuts we're facing."

APPROACHES TO INTERAGENCY COORDINATION

A number of attempts have been made to identify the various approaches to interagency coordination. We have sifted through these and organized them into *four chapters and twenty-two approaches within these chapters.* Generally, earlier chapters and earlier approaches within a chapter are easier than later ones, and the earlier forms of coordination often lead to the later forms. Undoubtedly you have experience with some of these already. You can use the tables that follow to assess your own agency's status in general or vis-à-vis each of the other agencies in your community with which you might coordinate. *Thus, the sections that follow give you not only an overview of approaches to interagency coordination and the remaining chapters of the guide, but also a picture of where you stand.*

BUILDING A SENSE OF COMMON PURPOSE

The first step in coordinating with other agencies is learning about them. Do you know *what* other education, employment, health, and social service agencies exist in your community, *how* each of them operates, *who* their typical clients are, *how many* clients they have or services they deliver? It's hard to coordinate with an agency about which you know nothing. Chapter 2 treats the approaches to building a sense of common purpose with other agencies. It also provides additional indicators to help you assess your current status on the various approaches.

Chapter 2—Building a Sense of Common Purpose

Number of Other Local Agencies
and Organizations Currently
Coordinated With in This Way
(check appropriate column)

	None	*Some*	*All*
1. Identifying potential benefits from coordination	____	____	____
2. Meeting with other agency administrators	____	____	____
3. Having your staff meet with other agency staff	____	____	____
4. Exchanging existing information with other agencies	____	____	____
5. Identifying obstacles to coordination	____	____	____
6. Developing plans to overcome obstacles	____	____	____
7. Establishing common objectives	____	____	____

MEETING IMMEDIATE CLIENT NEEDS

Once agencies have come to know and trust each other and have worked out some common objectives, the next level is coordination to meet typical client needs better. There are many approaches here, ranging from simple cross-referrals to various methods for coordinating efforts on groups of client cases to locating staff from two or more agencies in a common office. Chapter 3 treats these approaches.

Chapter 3—Meeting Immediate Client Needs

Number of Other Local Agencies
and Organizations Currently
Coordinated With in This Way
(check appropriate column)

	None	Some	All
1. Cross-referrals	____	____	____
2. Case consultation	____	____	____
3. Client conferences	____	____	____
4. Client teams	____	____	____
5. Case management by one agency	____	____	____
6. Colocation	____	____	____
7. Staff outstationing	____	____	____
8. Staff loans	____	____	____
9. Joint intake and assessment	____	____	____

MUTUAL GATHERING AND USE OF INFORMATION

There are lots of ways local agencies make use of information, from determining client health needs to tracking labor market trends and job openings. Chapter 4 treats approaches to coordinated gathering, organizing, and use of information required by such agencies.

INTEGRATED PROGRAM ADMINISTRATION

As coordination between agencies grows, eventually it reaches the point where not only services become integrated but administration of programs does also. This is the final level of interagency coordination. It includes such elements as joint program design, operation, and evaluation of cooperative programs. Chapter 5 treats this category of coordination.

Chapter 4—Mutual Gathering and Use of Information

Number of Other Local Agencies
and Organizations Currently
Coordinated With in This Way
(check appropriate column)

	None	Some	All
1. Organizing an information clearinghouse	____	____	____
2. Joint community needs assessments	____	____	____
3. Joint gathering of data to improve delivery of services	____	____	____

Chapter 5—Integrated Program Administration

Number of Other Local Agencies
and Organizations Currently
Coordinated With in This Way
(check appropriate column)

	None	Some	All
1. Joint program design	____	____	____
2. Joint program operation	____	____	____
3. Joint program evaluation	____	____	____

That's it. Twenty-two approaches to interagency coordination. If, as you proceed to learn more about these approaches, specific questions or concerns come to mind, the *annotated bibliography* of research reports and case studies on coordination located at the back of the guide may be helpful. Instructions for ordering copies of these materials are provided and the annotations make clear how each item complements what is presented here. The next section discusses resources that can be used in pursuing interagency coordination.

RESOURCES FOR INTERAGENCY COORDINATION

It is inevitable that, when one is faced with a new venture, an initial task is to identify the resources necessary to carry it out. This is called a *resources assessment.* As already mentioned, the administrative budget of any one agency is unlikely to provide all the resources for interagency coordination. *Nevertheless, there are such resources, as has been demonstrated time and again by imaginative agency administrators. Such resources may be found within agencies, within communities, and at the state and federal levels.* While assistance from more than one of these sources may be needed to support a given cooperative venture, most past efforts have originated at the local level and have relied heavily on local resources. The box that follows lists possible resources from all three sources; the discussion following the box provides examples and suggestions for each listed item.

Resource Sources

Resources within Local Agencies and Organizations

- Discretionary funds
- Personnel, materials, facilities, and other in-kind contributions
- Procedures and reward structures
- Agency advisory groups

Resources within Communities

- Local governing bodies
- Private interest groups and service organizations
- Businesses and industries

Resources at the State and Federal Levels

- Information-gathering agencies
- Technical assistance programs
- Grants and contracts

RESOURCES WITHIN AGENCIES

• *Discretionary funds.* Local agencies vary on how much control they have over the spending of their funds and how much of their budget is truly discretionary. However, even funds earmarked for a particular purpose or target population can often be used for related cooperative efforts. All that is required is flexibility and imagination—within agency regulations, of course.

• *Personnel, materials, facilities, and other in-kind contributions.* Work assignments can be changed to include interagency responsibilities. The reduction of duplicative activities through coordination may free up additional staff time. Materials and facilities can also be put to use to assist coordination efforts. For example, an empty office and some spare shelves can become a centralized interagency clearinghouse for information.

• *Procedures and reward structures.* Modify a procedure to emphasize *interagency* concerns and the resulting changes in behaviors of staff members can become a continuing force for coordination. Reward structures that promote interagency coordination cost little except imagination. Reward structures are the official and unofficial rules specifying which activities are disapproved and which activities are rewarded. Examples include job descriptions, promotion criteria, agency funding formulas based on caseloads, the ways numbers of clients or students are counted, and other requirements and incentives.

IDEA: Add to the existing employee performance-review process an assessment of efforts made to work with other agencies. Give especially active employees special recognition—an "interagent of the month" award, a plum assignment, a complimentary letter placed in the personnel files, . . .

• *Agency advisory groups.* These mandated bodies are often searching for meaningful roles to play. Help them identify ways they can support interagency coordination to improve client services. They can provide a rich source of ideas, contacts, and political support.

RESOURCES WITHIN COMMUNITIES

• *Local governing bodies.* Local officials can provide support for interagency cooperation by (1) directly funding pilot projects using locally generated or locally controlled monies, (2) indirectly supporting cooperative efforts through reallocation of the budgets of county agencies, or (3) writing letters of support to assist you in securing funds elsewhere.

• *Private interest groups and service organizations.* Chambers of commerce, Lions clubs, Rotary clubs, and many other civic service groups have been known to raise and donate funds for interagency efforts. They can also support your attempts at securing funds elsewhere. You might seek volunteer assistance from the local volunteer bureau or even from retired agency staff. Sometimes other community organizations already involved in cooperative planning are willing to help. For example, a local mental health organization might have the experience needed to help a department of corrections begin to cooperate with other community organizations.

In one large urban area, the combined efforts of several agency managers and representatives of the Rotary Club made it possible to present job-skills workshops for unemployed youth at several sites within the county. The workshops featured presentations by local employers and provided opportunities for the youth who attended to talk with interagency teams concerning available training programs.

• *Businesses and industries.* Representatives of local business and industry may be persuaded to provide money, in-kind contributions, political support, job-development programs, and help in attracting other businesses and jobs to the area.

Building a Business-Industry Constituency
for Interagency Coordination

1. Add business and industry representatives to agency and interagency planning groups.

2. Keep business and industry communities informed of agency and interagency activities through in-person presentations, workshops, newsletters, and personal contacts.
3. Establish a "hot line" or assign a staff person as a liaison so that employers can report their own employment and training needs and the health and counseling needs of their employees.
4. Make efforts to meet informally with individual employers to discuss community needs.
5. Volunteer to serve on business councils when the opportunity is presented.

RESOURCES AT THE STATE AND FEDERAL LEVELS

• *Information for local-level planning.* This is often available for the asking. If not tailored to the appropriate geographical area, it can be supplemented by canvassing of local data sources (such as an economic development center) and small-scale data-gathering efforts supported by local agency or community resources.

• *Technical assistance.* This is available for many geographical areas and types of agencies. Technical assistance providers represent important links to well-intentioned state programs, and working with them may increase the chances of receiving state support for cooperative ventures.

• *Grant and contract monies.* Learning how to express ideas and plans in terms that are responsive to the stated service goals of state and federal agencies is the key to preparing successful grant or contract applications to these agencies for support of interagency coordination among local service providers. There has been generally strong support for such efforts in recent years.

This is not an exhaustive listing of the resources that can be tapped for interagency coordination. Yet already it must be clear that, with a little creativity and organization, it is possible to garner resources for such efforts. The fact that interagency coordination is so fundamentally sensible gives it strong appeal to most people. Study after study has shown that if there is a will there is a way to make impressive achievements in this direction.

RECAP AND ATTITUDE QUIZ

Choices of how to proceed through this guide may be based on either your level of interest in these topics or your assessment of where your organization currently stands with respect to each category. If you are already expert on the topics in Chapters 2 and 3, for example, you can jump to later chapters. Alternatively, you may want to proceed systematically, chapter by chapter. As noted earlier, additional sources of information on interagency coordination are listed in the annotated bibliography at the back of the guide.

It is common to hear negative attitudes expressed when the possibility of agency changes is mentioned. This is the way most of us learn to react to the unfamiliar. We begin by citing all the reasons for *not* trying something different.

On pages 24-25 is a simple test of your general attitudes toward interagency coordination. Try it out and see how you score.

Chapter 2
Building a Sense of Common Purpose

1. Identifying potential benefits from coordination
2. Meeting with other agency administrators
3. Having your staff meet with other agency staff
4. Exchanging existing information with other agencies
5. Identifying obstacles to coordination
6. Developing plans to overcome obstacles
7. Establishing common objectives

Chapter 3
Meeting Immediate Client Needs

1. Cross-referrals
2. Case consultation
3. Client conferences
4. Client teams
5. Case management by one agency
6. Colocation
7. Staff outstationing
8. Staff loans
9. Joint intake and assessment

Chapter 4
Mutual Gathering and Use of Information

1. Organizing an information clearinghouse
2. Joint community needs assessments
3. Joint gathering of data to improve delivery of services

Chapter 5
Integrated Program Administration

1. Joint program design
2. Joint program operation
3. Joint program evaluation

What Are Your Attitudes Toward
Interagency Coordination?

Circle the number on each scale that best represents your attitude. Then add your ratings to learn your score on cooperativeness.

```
        1    2    3    4    5
        |----|----|----|----|
```

It took me a lot of
time and effort to
get things organized
the way they are.
Trying to coordinate
could disrupt the
organization I've
achieved in my agency.

There is always room for
improvement. Besides, I
like new efforts to make
things more effective
and efficient.

```
        1    2    3    4    5
        |----|----|----|----|
```

I know my staff and
co-workers and know
how to work with them.
And I know they're
good at what they do.
I don't know any of
these things about the
other agencies' staffs.

There are probably some
very interesting and
capable people in those
other agencies who can
teach me and my co-workers
some new things.

```
        1    2    3    4    5
        |----|----|----|----|
```

I don't have money
to pay for the things
I'm already trying to
do. How can I possibly
afford a new effort with
an undetermined payoff?

There should be relatively
little financial cost to
coordination, and it may
save me and my co-workers
some time and even some
money.

```
    1    2    3    4    5
    ├────┼────┼────┼────┤
```

How do I know what my
superiors will think of
such efforts? They may
come down on me for not
sticking to the agency's
business.

My higher-ups may like
this approach, see it as
showing initiative. There
has been a lot of emphasis
on better interagency
coordination at federal and
state levels in recent
years.

```
    1    2    3    4    5
    ├────┼────┼────┼────┤
```

I'm so swamped with
work already I simply
can't think about new
initiatives. I've got
to get out from under
the existing load first.

New cooperative initiatives
may actually ease the work
down a bit. This may be
one way to lift the load.

```
    1    2    3    4    5
    ├────┼────┼────┼────┤
```

This coordinated approach
entails some very real
risks. I find this
pressure to cooperate
irritating.

Not coordinating also in-
volves risks. Things will
always change. Do I want
to be seen as a leader or
a follower? This could be
an exciting and worthwhile
approach.

Scoring Key: 6-15 You have some strong reservations about interagency coordination. You need to read on to ease these doubts.

16-21 You have mixed feelings about this approach. Chapter 2 will help.

22-30 You are a natural candidate. The remainder of the guide is for you!

Chapter 2

BUILDING A SENSE OF COMMON PURPOSE

WHAT DO YOU KNOW ABOUT
OTHER AGENCIES?

It is surprising how little those working in one agency sometimes know about the functions of another agency in the same community. Who is the agency designed to serve? Where does its funding come from? What services does it offer? What are its eligibility requirements? Who should be contacted for referral when clients with particular needs appear? How do the services offered overlap with or complement the services of other agencies? All this is basic information about other community agencies—information that employees working in any one agency can use to benefit their clients.

You may be someone who is highly conversant with other agencies in your community. Alternatively, you may know some of the above information about some of the other agencies, but there may be gaps in your knowledge. The two exercises that follow provide a way for you to run a check on yourself in this respect. How much do you know about other agencies?

What Other Agencies Are There?

The first question is, Of what education, employment, health, and other social service agencies in your community are you aware? Consider:

- employment training agencies
- employment services offices
- rehabilitation agencies
- vocational education programs at high schools, colleges, regional occupational programs or centers, adult schools, and private vocational schools
- health and mental health agencies
- corrections agencies
- economic development agencies
- child and family services and agencies on aging
- welfare agencies
- community-based organizations (CBOs), community action agencies, chambers of commerce

Using these categories, make a list of all the agencies in your community you can think of. How many are there? Do you think this list is complete? How might you expand it, if not?

Do your responses on the next page suggest a comprehensive knowledge of the other organizations in your community? *A first step in any coordinated effort is to learn enough about other organizations to determine whether a coordinated effort would be possible and of interest.*

What Do You Know About Other Agencies?

Use the list of other agencies you just compiled. For how many of these agencies:

	None	Some	All
1. can you state their main goal or mission?	____	____	____
2. do you know the authority or legislation under which they operate (if any)?	____	____	____
3. do you know the sources and amount of their funding?	____	____	____
4. can you name the agency administrator?	____	____	____
5. do you personally know either the agency administrator or a staff member there?	____	____	____
6. can you describe the eligibility requirements for their clients (if any)?	____	____	____
7. do you know the approximate number of clients they serve annually?	____	____	____
8. can you describe the main services they offer?	____	____	____
9. can you describe the expertise represented on their staff?	____	____	____
10. can you describe the facilities and equipment they have?	____	____	____
11. do you have a phone number in your office or personal directory?	____	____	____
12. do you have a cross-referral system that is regularly used?	____	____	____
13. do you engage in any joint activities currently, other than cross-referrals?	____	____	____

IDENTIFYING POTENTIAL BENEFITS
FROM COORDINATION

Chapter 1 discussed in general terms the benefits of interagency coordination. All anticipated benefits are based on the principle of improving services to clients, of course. To accomplish this, we need to focus also on benefits to agencies, such as improving efficiency, expanding the resources available to an agency, and increasing the effectiveness of agency administrators. No two agencies are identical; each has needs of a particular variety and stands to gain from interagency coordination in particular ways. As an initial effort in exploring your interest in interagency coordination, it would probably be useful for you to figure out just what your agency stands to gain by coordinating with other agencies. You might ask a guest speaker from another community to present the benefits they have experienced. As a part of this, it would also be useful to identify what you have to offer other agencies in return. The exercise in the next box provides a starting point for such an assessment. Involving key administrators and staff in thinking about the benefits of coordination will help ensure that all the advantages are recognized.

In looking over your pattern of checks, what seem to be the most important needs of your agency that coordination with others might meet? What can you offer in return? With which other agencies in your community could your agency realize mutual benefits through coordination?

What You Can Gain or Provide Through
Interagency Coordination

	Your Agency Needs (check appropriate items)	Your Agency Has to Offer (check appropriate items)
Staff		
• Professional expertise on certain topics	____	____
• Staff with interests in certain types of clients	____	____

- Staff with particular skills (e.g., statistical, writing, counseling, testing, interviewing)
- Secretarial or clerical help _____ _____
- Other: _____ _____ _____

Equipment

- Typing _____ _____
- Duplicating _____ _____
- Word processing _____ _____
- Computer _____ _____
- Media-related (audiovisual) _____ _____
- Other: _____ _____ _____

Facilities

- Office space _____ _____
- Conference room _____ _____
- Counseling rooms _____ _____
- Office furniture _____ _____
- Advantageous location _____ _____
- Other: _____ _____ _____

Information

- On client needs _____ _____
- On community needs _____ _____
- Other: _____ _____ _____

Services

- Informational _____ _____
- Testing _____ _____
- Counseling _____ _____
- Treatment _____ _____
- Placement _____ _____
- Other: _____ _____ _____

Contacts

- With current and potential clients _____ _____
- With employers _____ _____
- With other agencies _____ _____
- With funding sources _____ _____
- With community leaders _____ _____
- With state or federal officials _____ _____
- Other: _____ _____ _____

MEETING WITH OTHER AGENCY
ADMINISTRATORS AND STAFF

Once you have zeroed in on those things you would most like to gain from coordinating with other agencies, as well as what you have to offer them in return, you can begin to think about which other agencies seem most likely to provide good matches. Which other agencies offer the services your clients could most use, and vice versa? Which other agencies have staff, facilities, or equipment you would most like to have access to, and vice versa? Information? Contacts? Perhaps most important, how do you feel about working with each agency? The quiz on the next page provides a way for you to assess this question for the other agencies in your community. A review of their "scores" should provide guidance in determining whether you are ready to coordinate with them. If you and your staff have strong negative feelings about another agency, you should try to become better acquainted with that agency before attempting more sophisticated forms of coordination.

If you are not familiar with another agency or have a negative impression of it, your first step should be making contact and getting acquainted. Someone has to take the initiative—if you don't, who will? The main objective of an initial contact is to open up a new line of communication. Past experience suggests it is wise not to try to accomplish lofty goals at first. The goal of getting to know another agency administrator and beginning to establish a comfortable relationship is central. Initial explorations of possible areas of coordination between the two agencies can occur, but they will only be preliminary to the subsequent meetings that

What Are Other Local Agencies Like?

This quiz is designed to help you determine how you and others on your staff feel about *particular agencies*. In the first exercise in this chapter, you listed the other local agencies and organizations in your community. Make copies of this quiz, filling in the names of those agencies (you may want your staff to do this also). Then fill out the following rating form for each agency. Of which agencies do you have high or low opinions?

Name of agency: _____

For each statement below, write in the number that describes how accurately you think the statement fits the agency.

> 1 = Disagree strongly
> 2 = Disagree slightly
> 3 = No opinion or don't know
> 4 = Agree slightly
> 5 = Agree strongly

1. _____ Their agency operations are too bureaucratic and inflexible for them to work cooperatively with us.
2. _____ Their staff are very professional, are well trained, and maintain high standards.
3. _____ Their clients often take unfair advantage of public funds.
4. _____ Their agency administrator and staff are friendly and welcome contact with other agencies.
5. _____ Many of their clients would be difficult for us to work with.
6. _____ They are quite willing to refer clients to us whenever we can serve the clients better than they can.
7. _____ They are only concerned with their agency's mission and don't pay sufficient attention to the needs of the entire community.
8. _____ If we developed a financial agreement with them, they could get the decision approved quickly by their supervisors or funding source.
9. _____ Their operations are affected too much by local politics for us to work well with them.

To score the quiz, follow this rule: Score = 21 + (sum of even-numbered ratings) - (sum of odd-numbered ratings). The scoring key is below.

Scoring Key: 0-4   Very low opinion of the agency;
                              cooperation probably impossible
                              until you get to know the agency
                              and its staff better.
                     5-13   Low opinion of the agency.
                     14-21   Neutral attitude—or maybe lack
                              of information?
                     22-30   High opinion of the agency;
                              coordination quite feasible.
                     31-36   You must be coordinating already!

will undoubtedly be necessary to follow up on such exploration. Thus, the following points should be kept in mind in making initial contacts:

- The main objective is to open up a new line of communication.

- Initial objectives related to interagency coordination are best if they are limited and low-risk in nature. It will take time for confidence to build, and this needs to occur before more ambitious, risky objectives are tackled.

- To allow confidence to build, some form of follow-up contact will be needed. Regular communication is essential to any interagency effort.

- Benefits to both agencies need to be clearly identified, so that each has a stake in the relationship.

- When interagency tasks are undertaken, they are best structured so that each agency has some responsibilities, and each can see that the other is doing its part. This "tit-for-tat" arrangement avoids early resentments from perceptions that one agency is doing less than the other and allows confidence to grow between the two agencies.

Initial contacts usually work best if they are between agency administrators, or at least if the request goes to the other agency administrator. This follows protocol and allows the other administrator to delegate the responsibility if he or she wishes. It avoids the problem of the administrator hearing about the contact from someone lower in the agency, becoming suspicious and defensive, and either scuttling the effort before it begins or putting it on an initial bad footing.

Once agency administrators have met and identified some initial possibilities for interagency cooperation, they should organize a similar meeting between some of their staff members. It will probably be the staff members who have to do much of the work and actual cooperating in an interagency effort, and involving them early will gain the benefit of their insights as well as the airing and resolving of any doubts about the relationship.

Meetings of agency staffs, like those of administrators, are usually best if they have limited objectives at first. Primarily, they are to exchange information on the two agencies and explore options for coordination. Just what information can be exchanged is the topic of the next section.

Possible Meeting Forums

There are a variety of forums for initial contacts and meetings between agency administrators and between agency staffs. Following are some suggestions.

Agency Administrators

1. Through a joint acquaintance

Agency Staffs

1. Through a meeting arranged at either office

2. Through some community activity or interest (service club, sport, church, etc.)

3. Through a conference

4. Through a meeting arranged at either office

5. For a breakfast, lunch, or after-work snack

2. Through a luncheon

3. Through a workshop on some aspect of interagency coordination

4. Through a late-afternoon office get-together

5. Through a sports activity (e.g., interoffice softball game, volleyball game)

EXCHANGING EXISTING INFORMATION

One of the easiest and most useful first steps in undertaking a coordinated effort with another agency is exchanging information that already exists. This costs each agency almost nothing; it simply extends the usefulness of work already done. Thus, identifying to what extent information can be usefully exchanged is one of the first topics for exploration with another agency's administrator and staff. Such information may be of two basic varieties: (1) that which pertains to the nature and operation of the agency itself, and (2) that which is useful in the delivery of services. A word about each of these follows.

The first thing one must know to coordinate with another agency is just what it is and does. One way of conveying such information is through handouts—brochures, leaflets, abstracts, or brief write-ups on an agency

that describe its basic functions. Every agency can easily develop such a handout and distribute it to other agencies. This can serve as the starting point for establishing cooperative relationships. The following is a list of the information about an agency that can be contained in such a piece.

THE AGENCY'S:

- Name, address, and phone number
- Basic purpose and objective
- Authority for existing (if any)
- Brief historical sketch (optional)
- Administrative structure (top administrator, main staff positions, any ties to a parent organization)
- Services offered (with perhaps a little detail for each type)
- Client eligibility rules (if any)
- Contact name and phone number for intake or referral

Of course, such handouts cannot address all the detailed questions that may arise. However, face-to-face meetings can flesh out the initial sketches and allow staff from both agencies to ask questions about the other and acquire as much detailed information as needed. For example, additional information can be provided on:

- the various services offered, such as timing, costs, and locations;
- eligibility requirements, unwritten rules about intended clients, special target groups;
- staff responsibilities at each agency—a brief description of the activities and duties of the various types of staff positions;
- staff abilities at each agency, such as specializations and particular skills; and
- administrative procedures.

A second type of information can also be exchanged almost from the beginning of an interagency contact. This is information related to the delivery of services. Included here is information about:

- client needs and characteristics (perhaps broken out by age, race, sex, socioeconomic status, or neighborhood);

- job-training programs (quality, timing, advantages/disadvantages of various options);

- placement services (such as those most effective with certain employers or in certain fields);

- economic and labor market information (such as local job demand in various fields, training and qualifications needed for such jobs, number of current applicants, unemployment rates, economic development plans);

- community health hazards and programs; and

- programs available for special populations (such as refugees, ex-convicts, homebound elderly)

In most instances, one agency will have better information than another on certain of these topics, and vice versa. By exchanging such information, both agencies can benefit and thereby improve their services. Mapping out and assigning the tasks necessary to allow such exchanges of information is usually one of the primary purposes of an early meeting between agency staffs.

Once initial exchanges of information have occurred, other means can be developed to keep such exchanges up-to-date. In-house reports can be circulated across agencies, regular meetings between key staff can be arranged, newsletters can be considered to keep all agency staff up-to-date. Also, interagency task forces can be formed to provide an established forum for pursuit of coordination; such task forces are discussed in a subsequent section of this chapter. Chapter 4 treats the more complex forms of joint information gathering and use such as organizing an information clearinghouse and conducting community needs assessments.

IDENTIFYING AND OVERCOMING
OBSTACLES TO COORDINATION

Reasons for not starting or continuing a cooperative venture can always be found, but five factors are the most frequent causes for agencies going it alone: *crisis operation, inflexibility, turfsmanship, bureaucracy,* and *politics.* These factors are powerful influences by themselves; in combination, they contribute to a pattern of resistance to change and business-as-usual approaches to delivering services. These can be devastating for the development of interagency perspectives and joint service delivery efforts.

Crisis Operation—Shrinking budgets, cutbacks in staff, and new community needs can make keeping their heads above water the number one priority of local administrators. Although common and understandable, crisis operation contributes to an unwillingness to consider alternative approaches, approaches that may be the very ones needed to break the cycle of crisis operation.

Inflexibility—Often little or no deviance is tolerated from an agency's rules and established operating procedures. Coordination requires a willingness to adapt to others' procedures. Flexibility, even for the larger good, may be difficult to come by in some agencies.

Turfsmanship—The belief that additional "turf" is needed to ensure agency survival can cause administrators to extend their service delivery approaches to the clientele of other agencies in the hope of expanding operations. Turfsmanship is the result of *competitiveness*, which is often counterproductive—especially for clients.

Competitiveness ≠ Productivity

Competitive reward structures do not necessarily lead to productive behavior. Studies have shown that cooperation generally leads to increased communication among participants, greater group cohesiveness, and higher levels of personal job satisfaction. In one study, an employment agency was used as an experimental setting. In one section of the agency, a job placement interviewer's job security depended on filling more job openings than other interviewers in the section. In another section, supervisors encouraged interviewers to develop a common purpose and make as many placements as possible without regard to their relative performance. Interviewers in the first section rarely talked with one another and actually concealed information about job openings. Those in the second section helped each other and learned to enjoy each other's company. More important, the cooperative section placed more job applicants!

Bureaucracy—Red tape often requires time—lots of time. The time required to have decisions approved at higher administrative levels may prohibit joint efforts among agencies. This can be a particularly troublesome problem for agencies with multiple levels of bureaucracy (such as district, state, and federal) and authoritarian decision-making structures.

Puncturing Bureaucracy

A productive interagency linkage that developed in one county would never have happened had ways not been found around bureaucratic red tape. The relationship involved the welfare and employment services offices and called for the stationing of welfare staff at the employment services office on a part-time basis. It was hoped that employment services staff would have an easier time referring needy clients to welfare staff. Likewise, welfare staff could learn of the procedures and regulations under which employment services staff worked, as well as find out about job openings of possible interest to their welfare clients. At first, attempts were made to negotiate a formal contract between the two agencies, an approach that required state-level approval. Problem after problem arose in granting such approval, however, due to various regulations. Finally, just when the project was about to be abandoned, the local agency administrators got together and worked out a nonfinancial cooperative arrangement that eliminated the need for a formal contract. The employment services office agreed to provide office space for the welfare staff, and the welfare department provided the required office furniture. The relationship has now lasted for several years and has been helpful both to the agencies and to their clients.

Politics—Out of the frying pan and into the fire! The more free your agency is of bureaucracy, the more subject it may be to the priorities imposed by federal, state, and local political issues. Conflicts among these priorities and competing political interests can stand in the way of any joint effort.

There are a variety of ways of dealing with these five obstacles to interagency coordination. The first is to *recognize their existence.* You can prepare yourself for dealing with them if you are aware of what the obstacles are and why they exist. You will be an exception if you don't have to deal with these problems somewhere in your attempts to foster interagency coordination.

A second step in dealing with such obstacles is to *focus attention on the overriding objective,* the greater good. If services really can be improved (and they can) through interagency coordination, find ways to show this to the turfists or bureaucrats who would stand in the way. If efficiency can be improved, illustrate how to the crisis-ridden administrator or issue-conscious local politician. If you have a better way, you have a powerful weapon on your side. It may take time to convince others, but with imagination and persistence it can be done.

A third means of overcoming obstacles is by *identifying key allies* in your struggle. There are almost always enlightened individuals working within other agencies who will be open to alternative approaches and will see the value of interagency coordination. Find them. Agency administrators are a good place to start, but don't be afraid to look up and down the bureaucratic ladder to find persons who can help get things done. The policymaking bodies and advisory boards often associated with public and private agencies are among the most powerful and strategically useful constituents for coordination efforts. These groups will eventually have to approve whatever interagency proposals are advanced, so it is best to involve them early and in the most constructive way possible in the coordination effort. Locate a few forward-thinking, articulate allies and you may find yourself overcoming obstacles faster than you thought possible.

Fourth, make use of *reward structures.* We all learn to operate in terms of reward structures, but there are likely to be few of these within a given agency to foster coordination efforts. Create some. Dream up a special award of some sort for engaging in cooperative efforts (a free dinner, an interesting business trip, a desirable assignment). One of the fastest, easiest, and least expensive ways of fostering new behavior is by creatively rewarding it. Make reward structures work for interagency coordination rather than against it.

This is not an exhaustive listing of ways to overcome obstacles to interagency coordination. What it does suggest is that it can be done. Experience has shown that obstacles will be encountered, as they are met in any attempt to promote change. Experience has also shown that they need not prevent change, if handled creatively. Achieving interagency coordination will require meeting a number of challenges. The same is true of any worthwhile venture.

Altering Reward Structures

An interesting experiment was done some years ago. It involved children from three types of communities—middle-class urban, poor urban, and poor rural. On each trial, four children from one of these communities sat at the corners of a square, holding a string that could be pulled to move a marking pen in the center. At first, children were rewarded for moving the pen through four target circles in sequence. This was a cooperative reward structure. On the next series of trials, however, each child received a reward only when the pen moved through his or her own circle. Cooperation was still the best strategy; if the children pulled against one another, chances were no one would receive many prizes. However, the reward structure was competitive.

What happened? On the first task, all groups cooperated, and all won numerous rewards. On the second task, however, the middle-class urban children became highly competitive and received fewer rewards than the rural and urban poor children, who continued to use a cooperative strategy. The experimenter attributed these differences to cultural background, noting that the poor children had learned to work together for family survival, whereas the middle-class children had parental models who competed in business.

ESTABLISHING COMMON OBJECTIVES

The goal of initial contacts with another agency (or agencies) is to establish a sense of common purpose, explore how the agencies might usefully coordinate their activities, and map out a plan of action for such coordination. The many forms this coordination may take are explored in the next three chapters. There are certain mutual understandings it is useful to have early in the process, however, such as the methods to be used to pursue coordination and agreements that state the common objectives of coordinating agencies and the contributions expected of each.

As initial efforts are made to explore possibilities for coordination between two agencies, the need will occur to establish some regular, ongoing form of contact to follow up initial meetings, allow responses to problems as they occur, and continue the process of defining the coordination desired. An approach commonly used toward this end is the establishment of an *interagency task force* with members from both agencies, or in the case of multiple-agency coordination, a planning body with representatives from all involved agencies. Such a group can provide a useful focus for coordination efforts and allow those interested in pursuing coordination to come together regularly in an established forum.

There are certain rules to follow in the establishment of an interagency task force:

Include all the potentially interested parties in authority. Those responsible for a significant program within an agency may resent not being consulted and obstruct efforts toward coordination if left out. Both in terms of numbers and authority, parity between (or among) agencies should be sought, to avoid intimidation or loss of enthusiasm on either side. At the onset, decide how community groups with vested interests or special interests can gain recognition and representation in the task force.

Limit the size of the task force or create an executive committee within a larger interagency group so that the body is of workable size. Twelve to fifteen represents an upper limit; fewer are better. It is a good idea to decide in advance on the procedures to be followed when adding new members or replacing members on the task force.

Designate individual responsibilities within the task force, among them a planning coordinator. Gathering and assembling the necessary information, as well as obtaining enough free time for members from their agency responsibilities, may represent problems for the task force. Leadership and individual commitment to the process will be needed. Subcommittees can also be established to investigate specific approaches. Be sure to define clearly the roles of task force members—whether they are to represent only one agency or a number of similar agencies, whether they are to be advocates for particular interest groups, whether they are to be experts in certain problem-related areas, and so on.

Avoid grandiose plans. Again, keep initial discussions limited and realistic. Once coordination and a good working relationship have been developed, plans can grow. Initially, it is far better to ensure small successes than to risk large disappointments.

THE REASON THE BOSS IS SENDING ME RATHER THAN YOU, HOSKINS, IS THAT HE PREFERS A SMALL SUCCESS TO A LARGE DISAPPOINTMENT.

Make it clear that the planning body will be only studying coordination and will have the power to recommend but not to decide. Final decisions will in most cases have to go back to the individual agencies.

The need for some formal agreement stating the nature and purposes of working arrangements agreed upon by two or more agencies varies from community to community. Some get along perfectly well without these; some prefer to have them. There are certain advantages to having them and certain ways of drawing them up, for those interested. Generally, such agreements are called *memoranda of agreement (MOAs) or memoranda of understanding (MOUs)*.

MOAs and MOUs are statements of the common objectives being sought through a coordinated effort. They usually also include a description of the roles and responsibilities for each cooperating agency. Their advantages are the following:

- They force the agencies to define their objectives and roles.
- They specify who is to take responsibility for managing and evaluating joint activities.
- They provide a reference point when future issues come up.
- They do not have to be legally binding and therefore can be modified easily as changes take place.
- They can usually be agreed to locally without formal approval by the agencies' funding sources.
- They represent an initial symbol of the goodwill and intended cooperation between the agencies involved.

An example of a cover statement for an MOU follows. As indicated in this statement, descriptions of the scope of service to be coordinated and the responsibilities of the two cooperating agencies would also be included in the agreement. These would take up two or three additional pages in the MOU (not included here).

While MOUs and MOAs generally contain a definition of common objectives in some form, an alternative is simply to draw up a list of such common objectives. This may lack some of the formal and symbolic quality of the usual written agreement, but it does accomplish the basic purpose of mapping out the objectives to be sought through the coordinated effort. In one county, twenty-nine providers of employment and training services came together to coordinate their efforts. Calling themselves the "Employment and Training Providers Clearinghouse," they drew up a set of twelve common objectives they would pursue. These are listed on page 46.

Memorandum of Understanding

between

MOUNTAIN COUNTY
MANPOWER CONSORTIUM   and   VALLEY DEPARTMENT OF
REHABILITATION
Hereinafter CETA   Hereinafter VDR

Effective Date of Agreement: April 12, 1982

WHEREAS, the Mountain County Manpower Consortium and the Valley Department of Rehabilitation are the two major deliverers of vocational services for the handicapped in Mountain County.

WHEREAS, the State Department of Rehabilitation is a state agency providing services to handicapped individuals.

WHEREAS, the Mountain County Manpower Consortium has been duly constituted under the Comprehensive Employment and Training Act of 1973 (as amended) to provide CETA programs within Mountain County.

Therefore, this Memorandum of Understanding is entered into by and between the Mountain County Manpower Consortium (hereinafter referred to as CETA) and the Valley Department of Rehabilitation (hereinafter referred to as VDR). It is not the intention of the parties that this Memorandum of Understanding should create any legally enforceable rights or obligations, and it is expressly declared that this is not a contract, agreement, or any other legally binding document. The parties desire to state in written form what areas of interest the two agencies have in common so that the parties may be better able to coordinate delivery of services. This Memorandum of Understanding shall consist of the following parts:

Part I	Scope of Service
Part II	VDR Responsibilities
Part III	CETA Responsibilities

MOUNTAIN COUNTY MANPOWER CONSORTIUM

BY: *Jane A. Leader*

TYPED NAME: Jane A. Leader

TITLE: Area Manpower Administrator

DATE: 4-12-82

VALLEY DEPARTMENT OF REHABILITATION

BY: *John B. Friendly*

TYPED NAME: John B. Friendly

TITLE: Regional Director

DATE: 4-12-82

Summary of the Purposes of the
Employment and Training Providers Clearinghouse

1. Identify employment and training provider agencies.

2. Identify resources in each agency.

3. Establish an informal forum to maximize usage of local resources.

4. Identify those occupations most in demand in the county.

5. Identify which demanded occupations need to have training programs developed.

6. Analyze which existing training programs should provide additional training services.

7. Discuss which agencies in the county might best provide those training services.

8. Identify the number of successful completers in each program.

9. Establish a forum to develop linkages and interagency agreements for services integration to provide better services to clients and reduce duplication.

10. Assist in the development of formal agreements between agencies via contracts and memoranda of agreement and understanding (MOAs and MOUs).

11. Assist in identifying sources of funding to aid employment and training supportive services.

12. Identify areas for further research (e.g., studies of joint placement programs, involvement of the private sector, or economic development).

Establishing interagency task forces and drawing up memoranda of agreement or understanding are two means toward achieving the end of building a sense of common purpose between agencies. They follow the earlier steps discussed in this chapter: learning about other agencies, identifying specific benefits from interagency coordination for your agency, meeting with other agency administrators and staff, exchanging existing information, and identifying and overcoming obstacles to coordination. *A strong sense of common purpose is fundamental if an interagency effort to achieve coordination is to reach fruition.* It represents a foundation on which to build. Once such a foundation exists, there are many forms the coordination can take. These are presented in the chapters that follow.

Chapter 3

MEETING IMMEDIATE CLIENT NEEDS

HOW DO YOU DO MORE
FOR LESS?

Meeting the immediate needs of students, persons with disabilities, the unemployed, employers, children, families, the elderly, and other clients is not easy. This is particularly the case in periods of diminishing resources. There are, however, several ways to do this when the agencies in a community build on each other's strengths. One specific approach that your agency probably uses already is a system of cross-referrals. Because referrals are easiest to implement (and easiest to improve), we begin discussion in this chapter with them, specifically with the cross-referral checklist on the next page.

MAKING THE REFERRAL
PROCESS WORK

The patterns of checks and circles on the Cross-Referral Checklist are indicators of what use you are making of this interagency approach to meeting client needs. Read through the questions listed below, look over your checklist, and consider where the strengths and weaknesses are.

• Are you referring clients to more agencies than are referring to your agency (more checks in the left-hand column)? Would you like to be serving more referrals from these agencies?

Cross-Referral Checklist

For each type of local agency listed below (except for your own, of course), consider the referrals you make and receive from the agency. Put checks in the spaces provided to indicate whether you regularly refer to or receive referrals from the agency.

	Refer to	*Receive* *Referrals from*
Employment training agencies	_____	_____
Employment services offices	_____	_____
Rehabilitation agencies	_____	_____
Vocational education programs at:		
high schools	_____	_____
colleges	_____	_____
regional occupational programs or centers	_____	_____
adult schools	_____	_____
private vocational schools	_____	_____
Health and mental health agencies	_____	_____
Corrections agencies	_____	_____
Economic development agencies	_____	_____
Child and family services and agencies on aging	_____	_____
Welfare agencies	_____	_____
Community-based organizations (CBOs), community action agencies, chambers of commerrce	_____	_____

NOW, GO BACK AND TAKE A CLOSER LOOK. Wherever you made a check, ask yourself whether as many clients as can be served effectively are being referred (i.e., not too many or too few). If so, draw a circle around the check.

- How often are your referral relationships with other agencies *cross-referral* arrangements (checks in both columns for single agencies)?

- In how many cases are about the right number of clients (not too few or too many) being referred who are eligible for services from the receiving agency (numbers of circles relative to the numbers of checks)?

- Are many of your agency's cross-referral relations operating at the most effective levels—that is, are as many clients referred back and forth as can be provided quality services (circled checks in both columns for single agencies)?

- How well do you know the number of referrals your staff are making and how many referrals your agency is receiving? (Would other staff in your agency fill out the checklist differently?)

IMPROVING REFERRALS

Whether you are concerned that people in need find out that you exist or concerned about the productivity of your agency, referrals from other agencies and organizations are important. You don't want too many or too few referrals, and persons referred should be eligible for your programs. If you are not getting the numbers and types of referrals you would like, consider whether your agency is referring clients properly to other agencies. Are there as many checks in the right-hand column of the checklist as there might be? How many of these checks have circles drawn around them? When you do not refer to others when they could effectively serve your clients, how can you expect them to refer the right clients to you?

If your answers are "yes, we refer clients to a variety of other service providers" and "yes, we refer only as many clients as those agencies can handle effectively" and you are still receiving fewer eligible referrals than you would like in return, consider whether you have effectively used your referrals as a *leverage tool*. Have you personally called the attention of other agency administrators to the use you are making of the referral process with their agencies? Do you routinely keep them apprised of the service capabilities of your agency and your interest or (forced) lack of interest in serving additional clients? Personal contact, reasonable pressure, and routine reminding are helpful strategies in achieving a balance between referrals and service capabilities.

> **IDEA**: Make up a form letter (but be sure *you* write in the other administrator's name and sign your own each time it is sent out) that advises the other agency administrators of the referrals you have made to them in the past month and reviews your agency's service capabilities.

If you *have* sought to remind the administrators of other agencies that you are being conscientious in your referrals to them and *still* your incoming referrals are not what you would like (too many, too few, too many ineligible), the problem may be the result of poor communications between administrators and staff in these agencies. With the administrator's support, you might try the following approach for communicating directly with another agency's staff.

> **IDEA**: Put together a flyer that reminds agency staff to refer clients to your agency for certain specialized services, and ask that it be posted where staff can't miss it.

DEVELOPING CROSS-REFERRAL RELATIONSHIPS

Cross-Referral Network = Two-Way Referrals + Coordination

When your agency and another agency in the community regularly refer clients back and forth, you have a cross-referral relationship. While this is a good sign, it *can* be improved upon. Specifically, you can build your cross-referral system into an established *cross-referral network*. Let's look at the basic components of this type of network.

Agency brochures and *multiagency directories* can be of use in keeping track of the service capabilities of other agencies and organizations in the community. These materials are especially helpful for orienting staff with regard to the purposes, general service capabilities, and eligibility requirements of other agencies when they are regularly updated to reflect changes in regulations or procedures and are supplemented by direct contacts among agency staffs.

Regular meetings of agency administrators and *interagency staff workshops* held periodically to estimate service needs and capabilities can also serve to initiate and maintain a cross-referral network. If once a month is too often to expect changes in service capabilities, hold meetings every two or three months, and use these meetings to introduce and reacquaint staff from the different agencies. When staff are informed of what other agencies can provide, they are much more likely to know which clients to send to which agencies when the need arises.

Finally, a *record-keeping system for referrals* can be an important aid to monitoring the performance of a cross-referral network. The essential elements for such a system are *easy-to-follow procedures* and *staff incentives* to encourage monitoring of the referral process. Close coordination in tracking clients and matching their needs to available services can easily lead to joint intake and assessment procedures for two or more agencies (to be discussed later in this chapter).

REDUCING FRAGMENTATION OF
CLIENT SERVICES

Clients with multiple needs are often on their own in learning about and wading through the bureaucracies of the local agencies that can help them. At times they may feel like a tennis ball bounced back and forth between agencies (if they are lucky enough to be referred to another agency at all).

Each visit to a new agency means that the person in need has to start all over again describing his or her problems and preferences and filling out forms on background and qualifying information. After enduring the troubles involved in making the trip and the embarrassments of disclosing personal needs, many clients will be found to be ineligible for services. Even if a client *is* eligible to receive services, service plans are often drawn up by one agency without regard for any services the client may be receiving from other agencies. This lack of planning about the full range of services that a client and his or her family may need and the lack of coordination of services that are provided by different agencies is known as "fragmentation" or "lack of continuity." *Interagency coordination can ease this difficulty by treating a client as a whole person, not as an assortment of unrelated problems.*

In addition to causing frustration for clients and staff and often leaving some needs unmet, fragmentation of client services can also cause the services that are supplied to be less effective. Sometimes clients are sent through a training program but are given insufficient help in landing a job when they complete the course. Other times clients are eligible for a training program but do not participate fully because of a health or mental health problem or because they do not know how to find or afford a day-care center, transportation, an interpreter for the deaf, or some other support service. Situations such as these bring to mind an important management concept: *protection of investment.* A client often needs one service in order to take full advantage of another service. The agency to which the client has applied for assistance will therefore be protecting its investment if it makes sure that the client receives both services. Four approaches to interagency coordination—*case consultation, client conferences, client teams, and case management—can all reduce fragmentation, increase continuity for clients, and thereby protect the individual investments by agencies serving a community.*

CASE CONSULTATION AND CLIENT CONFERENCES

Case consultation simply involves staff at one agency asking advice from staff at another agency about particular clients. The questions may pertain to whether the client is eligible for certain services, what services a mutual client is already receiving, or which program is most appropriate for this client. No matter what the question, *the purpose is to pool the professional knowledge about the case at the two agencies and to coordinate the services that are provided.* Case consultation is as easy as picking up the phone (if you know whom to call), but in spite of its ease, it is a form of interagency coordination that is frequently neglected. Many staff are shy about calling an unknown person in an unknown agency, which is why interagency visits and periodic staff meetings are important for keeping case consultation a regular part of cooperation between the agencies. As an agency administrator, you can frequently check that your staff are consulting other agency staff when they need information. If they are not, you should take steps to encourage greater interaction.

Client conferences are only slightly more organized than case consultations, but the potential payoffs are greater for the efficiency of the agencies involved. In a client conference, staff from two or more agencies discuss the needs of all the clients they have in common at a single meeting. *Because the staff from both agencies are asking and answering questions, all involved will benefit from the exchange of information, and there is greater likelihood that all of the clients' major problems will be addressed at one time.* With a little encouragement and urging from agency administrators, case consultations can easily turn into client conferences, and before you know it, coordination is taking place without anyone even saying the word!

Supporting Case Consultation
and Client Conferences

1. Give each of your staff a one-page list of the names and phone numbers of contact persons in other agencies (by program within the agency, when the programs are staffed separately).

2. Routinely ask clients about other agencies they have gone to recently, contact the other agency to explore how the delivery of services might be coordinated, and suggest to the client how the two agencies might be able to pool resources to provide assistance.

3. Let your staff know that the conference room can be used to meet with staff from other agencies to discuss the needs and welfare of a number of mutual clients.

4. Assist your staff with transportation to meet with staff in another agency (e.g., reimburse travel costs).

CLIENT TEAMS

Client teams are the next step after client conferences. A client team is made up of staff from two or more agencies who coordinate their activities to meet the needs of a number of clients through continuous and systematic interaction. Client teams are often formed for clients who will be needing services over a relatively long period of time or who have many severe needs, but this is not necessarily the case. *Agencies can use client teams to make the intake process more efficient* (for example, where groups of clients initially meet with the team rather than going from one agency to the next) and to reduce fragmentation and duplication of services. Another advantage is that *the client is always dealing with the same team of two or three staff members and can assume that this team is already familiar with his or her case.* Unlike client conferences, client teams usually interact on a regular basis (possibly even the same day each week).

HOSKINS, WHY ARE YOU THE ONLY ONE WHO TOOK ME SO LITERALLY WHEN I SAID WE'D ORGANIZE CLIENT TEAMS...?

An Example of Client Teams

The welfare department and one of the employment services offices in a county set up joint client teams for welfare applicants capable of working. New welfare applicants were sent to the employment services office on either of two specified mornings each week, and Work Incentive (WIN) eligibility workers at the employment services office and social workers from the welfare department were there to orient them to the requirements and services of the WIN program. An initial group session was held in a conference room, and an overhead projector was used to illustrate procedures and features of the program. This group session was followed by an individual session for each applicant with a client team made up of a social worker and a WIN eligibility worker. The effects of the system were quite positive. Clients learned more about the range of services WIN had to offer, the registration session was more efficient because it took place at one location and all questions were answered at one time, and a closer relationship developed between the WIN eligibility workers and the social workers.

Another Example of Client Teams

In a recent educational demonstration program, client teams were located in offices at participating schools. Team members worked together and communicated frequently throughout the day. Each client team was made up of a social worker, a rehabilitation counselor, an employment services specialist, and a vocational counselor from the school. Students who appeared to be in need of some social service were assigned to one of the client teams. The client team would periodically meet with the student and with his or her parents, if need be, as long as the student continued to require counseling or other assistance. During evaluation of the system, students were randomly assigned to either a client team, a case manager (described in the next section), or the traditional counseling office in the school. Participants in both of the coordinated approaches received more services and a greater range of services than did students in the traditional group. In addition, all the cooperating agencies shared credit for each student who was helped.

Organizing Client Teams

1. Draw up a memorandum of agreement with one or more agencies to set up client teams.

2. Have the teams meet on a regular schedule, and reserve a room for them on those days.

3. Explore ways that the teams could be located at the same office (another agency's or yours) at least one day each week. Client teams can operate even more effectively when combined with outstationing of this sort.

CASE MANAGEMENT

Fragmentation of services is caused by no one taking the responsibility to see that a client gets through the bureaucratic mazes within and between agencies. In the three forms of coordination just discussed, staff from several agencies share this responsibility. *In case management, staff at one agency are given responsibility for coordinating the services provided by several agencies to meet the needs of particular clients.* They represent these clients when contacting other agencies and serve as advocates for the client if there are any misunderstandings.

This much of case management is not uncommon. To further interagency coordination and to make the case managers as effective as possible, however, *the case management role of one agency should be agreed to by the other agencies.* Preferably, a memorandum of agreement should be drawn up that specifies which kinds of clients the agency is to manage and what the responsibilities of all the agencies are in those cases. In addition, the case managers should be given special training by staff in the other agencies concerning eligibility requirements, regulations, required forms and other documentation, and so on. With these additional procedures, case management by a single agency can become an excellent form of interagency coordination.

An Example of Case Management

Usually, case managers are staff in one of the main public agencies (for example, rehabilitation counselors often serve as case managers for their handicapped clients), but there have been some notable exceptions. The community action agency (CAA) in one county found itself often trying to help clients who were having problems with welfare aid. An agreement was worked out by which the welfare department would train several of the staff at the CAA to be welfare client advocates. The idea was that, if staff could be taught the details of the welfare regulations and procedures, they could then provide accurate information to such clients and help to work out any problems that came up. After they had completed the training, regular meetings were held between the client advocates and the welfare director to seek ways to improve the functioning of the department. As time passed, the staff at the CAA became knowledgeable about eligibility requirements at a number of other local agencies, and eventually they found themselves serving as case managers. For each of their clients, they would take responsibility for guiding the person through the procedures of whichever health or social service programs matched that person's needs, and, when necessary, they served as advocates for their clients in clearing up misunderstandings with the other agencies. Fragmention of the services supplied to their clients was greatly reduced, and the other agencies benefited from having the external client advocates be well informed about agency regulations.

Making Case Management Work

1. Get the name of the person handling the cases in the other agency, and check back periodically.

2. Be careful not to sound demanding when calling another agency about your clients. Instead, suggest ways that you can help the other agency, and emphasize how their services and your services are more effective for the clients when combined.

3. Meet with administrators of other agencies periodically to explore how your role as case manager could be made more effective and efficient for all concerned.

WHAT DOES YOUR AGENCY DO TO REDUCE FRAGMENTATION OF CLIENT SERVICES?

On the next page is a checklist much like the one on cross-referrals presented earlier. The same types of agencies are listed down the side, and the types of coordination we have just been discussing are listed across the top. The patterns of checks and circles after you fill it out are indicators of the ways in which your agency is helping to reduce fragmentation of client services and with whom. They also indicate *opportunities for improvement—which new forms of coordination you might consider trying, which current procedures could be encouraged more or made official, and with which additional service providers you might consider cooperating for the sake of your clients and theirs.* After patting yourself on the back for being so coordinated already, you might want to consider whether any of the blanks or uncircled checks represent areas for further work.

Checklist for Reducing Fragmentation
of Client Services

For each type of local agency listed below (except your own, of course), consider in what ways you ensure continuity of services for your mutual clients. *Put checks in the spaces provided to indicate if your staff sometimes engages in these forms of coordination.*

	Case Consultation or Client Conferences	*Client Teams*	*Case Management* *(by your agency)*	*(by the other agency)*
Employment training agencies	____	____	____	____
Employment services offices	____	____	____	____
Rehabilitation agencies	____	____	____	____
Vocational education programs at:				
high schools	____	____	____	____
colleges	____	____	____	____
regional occupational programs or centers	____	____	____	____
adult schools	____	____	____	____
private vocational schools	____	____	____	____
Health and mental health agencies	____	____	____	____
Corrections agencies	____	____	____	____
Economic development agencies	____	____	____	____
Child and family services and agencies on aging	____	____	____	____
Welfare agencies	____	____	____	____
Community-based organizations (CBOs), community action agencies, chambers of commerce	____	____	____	____

NOW GO BACK AND TAKE A CLOSER LOOK. Wherever you made a check, *draw a circle around the check if your staff have been told that this particular coordination is encouraged.* Then for each circle, *draw a second circle around the check if this interagency relationship has been encouraged or spelled out in writing* (for example, as a memo circulated to your staff or as a memorandum of understanding).

INCREASING THE ACCESSIBILITY OF CLIENT SERVICES

Just as multiagency coordination can reduce the fragmentation of client services, planning and carrying out program-related activities with other agencies can make services more available to clients. *Four approaches that are often used to increase the accessibility of services to those in need are colocation, outstationing, staff loans, and joint intake and assessment.* The first three of these involve the relocation of staff either temporarily or on a longer-term basis. The fourth approach requires that two or more agencies determine the commonalities in their requests of information from clients and find a way to collect and share this information more efficiently.

COLOCATION, OUTSTATIONING, AND STAFF LOANS

Colocation involves two or more agencies having staff and separate facilities at the same location. While this working arrangement may not be suitable for some community programs (such as vocational education offerings in high schools), it is often relatively easy to arrange and can substantially reduce the problems clients may have in obtaining assistance. Clients can visit both agencies with little extra effort, and the close proximity of the agencies makes possible closer staff interaction and encourages cross-referrals and the formation of client-centered, integrated service procedures (such as client teams). Beyond the initial selection of a service site and the arrangement of (separate) office facilities, however, colocation may not require any additional interagency planning or coordination of services. Colocation presents opportunities for coordination; it is up to the agency administrators and staff to take advantage of those opportunities.

An Example of Colocation, Outstationing, and Joint Intake and Assessment

A community facility in one county currently houses six colocated agencies and programs:

1. Social Services Division (income maintenance and social services programs),
2. Public Health Services,
3. Urban League (employment training program),
4. Neighborhood Service Center (community-based information and referral unit),
5. Employment Services Office, and
6. Work Incentive Program (WIN).

In addition, several other programs are outstationing staff at this facility on a regularly scheduled basis:

7. Youth Employment Program,
8. County Rehabilitation Services, and
9. Office of the District Attorney.

Service specialists, working with all the agencies, guide clients through emergencies, simple information requests, service needs identification, service plan development, referrals, case management functions, and follow-up interviews. A dozen different initial inquiry and application forms have been consolidated into a single form, which is provided to clients by the service specialists. These specialists also have access to information provided by the county's management information system that allows them to track clients through multiple agencies.

Colocation: Challenges and Responses

Challenge: "We can't afford to move."

Response: Be prepared to detail the benefits that can be expected from the move of some or all staff to the new location (e.g., increase in clients applying for services). Point out that the whole agency need not relocate. At first, suggest that only a counselor and a secretary be assigned to the colocated site and be regarded by the parent agency as a branch office. Ask the administrator to describe what costs would still be too great, and see if a meeting can be arranged with his or her regional administrator to discuss what can be done.

Challenge: "All our staff need to be in close contact with one another, not spread all over the county."

Response: Point out that telephones will be readily available at the new site and that meetings between main office and colocated staff can be held regularly. Note that the colocated facility will permit staff at the site to be in contact with many other kinds of professionals working on similar problems.

Challenge: "We need all the staff we've got at our main office to serve our daily client load."

Response: Sit down with the administrator and try to establish just where the current clientele is drawn from. See where the colocated facility is in relation to these sources, and point out that the client load at the main office could very well be reduced because clients will find it easier to reach the colocated facility.

Outstationing means that staff from one agency are sent to work in the facilities of another agency. Because staff will be using *another agency's facilities,* coordination among the participating agencies is essential for the success of an outstationing effort. Written agreements, such as memoranda of understanding, are especially important for clarifying just what facilities are to be provided by the host agency and what responsibilities are to be met by the outstationed staff persons. You will want other agency staff to understand, for example, that although your staff are located at their facility, you are still counting on them to provide services in accordance with your agency's primary mission.

Suggestions for Outstationing Staff

1. In selecting staff to be sent to work in other agencies, consider their abilities to get along with co-workers, to adjust to changes in the work environment, and, generally, to take a positive attitude when faced with new challenges. Sometimes staff selections are based solely on abilities to process many clients efficiently, time

availability, or on geographical considerations (e.g., it would be a shorter commute for some staff if they were reporting to a different site), with the unfortunate result that the staff chosen for outstationing are ill-equipped for the new work situation.

2. Set aside time to thoroughly familiarize the staff to be out-stationed with the personnel and work routines of the other agencies. If possible, organize visits to the sites and consider whether the outstationing assignment can be carried out in stages (e.g., from part-time to full-time assignment on a gradual basis). Provide your staff with the names and descriptions of persons in the other agency with whom they will work in close proximity. Similarly, assist your staff in planning transportation to the agency.

3. Work with the administrators of the other agencies to organize one or more orientation sessions for the staff who are to be working in the same facility. Also, take the time to work out supervisorial responsibilities with other agency administrators. Be clear about what directions you will be providing to your staff and what areas of supervision you expect other administrators to take charge of.

Staff loans result in staff from one agency working under the direct supervision of another agency and on tasks assigned by that agency for a temporary period. Staff loans differ from outstationing in that the staff are assigned to work *for the other agency,* albeit on a short-term basis. These loans sometimes represent interagency responses to one agency's call for additional staff assistance (as a result of unexpected budget cuts, for example). Alternatively, staff loans are sometimes used to increase the experience and skill levels of staff by exposing them to new work environments. A primary purpose of staff loans in either case, however, is to have staff understand the other agency better and to enable the two agencies to work more closely together.

Staff Loans at the State Level

The transfer of staff persons among different agencies at the state level is currently being used in one western state as an approach to building staff and agency capabilities. "Administrators-on-loan," as program participants are known, are assigned to another agency where they learn firsthand about the objectives and procedures that are followed. More important, these staff persons have the opportunity to meet and develop working relationships with the supervisors and staff in the new agencies to which they are assigned. Periodically, participants involved in the on-loan program meet to discuss what they are learning about the different agencies to which they have been assigned and to explore new areas for interagency coordination either at the state or local level. Because of their distinctive interagency perspectives, acquired through the on-loan program, these staff frequently are called upon to review proposals, attend meetings, and work with local-level staff with an eye to finding greater opportunities for interagency cooperation.

Whether staff loans are used to improve interagency coordination, to bolster another agency's resources temporarily, or to promote staff development, these staff arrangements are best entered into with a clear understanding of what each agency expects from the other. It is a good idea to prepare a written statement of what all participating agencies will provide to and expect from the staff loan arrangement.

Staff Outstationing and Staff Loans: Challenges and Responses

Challenge: "Our staff have altogether different training and professional backgrounds from yours."

Response: Mention that federal and state agencies have for years used staff loan and exchange programs to increase staff knowledge and skills. Talk about what both agency staffs will be learning, and stress that a likely result will be closer working relationships in the future.

Challenge: "To send staff to your agency will leave us short-handed."

Response: Suggest that you could send them some of your staff to handle the load. You can turn a request for staff out-stationing or loan into a staff exchange. Perhaps another agency with greater staff resources will have to be involved to help meet the immediate problem of client overload, but then you have turned a bilateral activity into a multiagency one.

The checklist below is designed to start you thinking about whether colocation, outstationing, or staff loans might be of use to your agency. If any of the statements on the checklist are true for your agency, consider some of the suggestions presented in the troubleshooting key (following the checklist) for improving the accessibility of services to clients.

Checklist of Service Accessibility

Read the statements below and check whether what is described in each case is true for your agency.

1. When we refer clients to other agencies, they frequently complain that transportation to the agency will be a problem.

   True   False

2. We probably lose a lot of referrals because clients either cannot get to our agency or do not bother to make the trip.

   True   False

3. Clients that are referred to our agency often are not eligible for our services.

   True   False

4. Some of our staff make it a habit not to refer to certain other agencies because they have little respect for staff in those agencies.

   True   False

5. We have gotten into a rut when it comes to working with clients and could use some fresh ideas.

   True   False

**Troubleshooting Key for the Checklist
of Service Accessibility**

1. *True*—Short of providing transportation for clients out of your own budget, you may want either (a) to invite the other agency to *outstation* someone at your office one or two days a week, or (b) to consider a *colocation* arrangement with the agency if a cross-referral relationship has already been established and is operating effectively.

2. *True*—If the problem arises with one or two agencies, try *outstationing* a staff person in each agency one or two days a week to screen prospective clients. If the problem is with many agencies, you are located in the wrong place (e.g., too far out of the city), and perhaps a more centrally located *branch office* should be opened.

3. *True*—Two approaches might be tried here. First, consider *outstationing* staff in those agencies responsible for the largest number of referrals. Second, why not suggest that selected *staff from these agencies be loaned to your agency* for two weeks to a month to learn what services are provided and which procedures must be followed.

4./5. *True—Loaning staff* from your agency to one or more other agencies on a short-term, rotating basis would help. Consider these individuals to be "on loan to learn." You might want to see how interested other agency administrators would be in setting up a *staff exchange program* to help agencies and staff learn from one another. (This approach would also help to quiet concerns that loans of staff out of the agency lessen the number of staff available to handle the daily client load.)

JOINT INTAKE AND ASSESSMENT

Joint intake and assessment occur when agencies use a common system for screening clients and diagnosing their needs. A centralized intake point for employment and training providers in the community, for example, is one way to streamline service procedures. A client would go to this intake point (the office of one agency designated to meet and refer clients initially) and provide information on a single form that would then be shared by the agencies to which the client is referred. In this way, the client would be freed from repeatedly answering similar questions posed in different ways on different agency application forms. Because a centralized intake system is usually more workable *after* agencies have colocated their facilities, communities wishing to begin joint intake and assessment often start with the development of a common intake or client application form. Each of the local agencies then uses the form when initially screening clients, asks their permission to release the information to other agencies, and shares the information with whichever other agencies the client is advised to visit. This is known as *uniform record-keeping.*

Joint Intake and Assessment:
Challenges and Responses

Challenge: "Our agency's regulations require that we collect all client information on our own form."

Response: Usually this objection is well justified. Regulations for uniform data collection and reporting can create problems. The best approach is to try to lobby for waivers of certain regulations to allow your coordinated intake and assessment procedure to be tried. You will either be able to get some rules waived, find that some items of information on the mandated forms can be shared among the other agencies, or conclude that some agencies will just have to use their own forms in addition to filling out the joint intake and assessment materials.

Challenge: "We are all going to need to copy the information over anyway, for our own records, and then try to match this information with the more specific items we will have to collect from clients on our own."

Response: This is really a paper-management problem that is best tackled as soon as it becomes apparent that some agencies will not be allowed to waive the use of their mandated forms. Point out that staff in the agency will have to take responsibility for seeing to it that a copy of a client's joint intake and assessment form is filed together with his or her agency-specific form. Staff should also be told to refer to the joint form for information that is also recorded on the agency-specific form rather than to ask clients for the same information all over again.

Joint Intake and Assessment:
Another Challenge and Response

Challenge: "Without automation—some sort of computer that we can all use—a joint intake and assessment system is just not feasible."

Response: Automation can be a real asset, but it is not essential. For example, an intake and assessment form that meets some or all of the agencies' client information needs can be developed, used by the agency first contacted by the client, and then passed from one agency to the next as the client is referred to other services. There are several ways to accomplish this:

First, the client could hand-carry it from agency to agency. This does place the responsibility on the client, however, and sometimes results in loss of the form.

Second, an agency can mail the form to the next agency, keeping a copy for its records. This is more efficient, and there is less likelihood that the form will be lost. However, even local mails often take two days for delivery, and without further controls, the client is apt to appear for services at an agency before the filled-out form arrives. A better approach appears to be one in which the agency to whom the filled-out form is sent takes responsibility for calling the client and scheduling an appointment. In this case, no appointments are made by the new agency until the forms are received.

Third, if staff frequently go back and forth between agencies (e.g., for outstationing or client team meetings), they could serve as couriers and deliver copies of the forms to the next agency without waiting for mail delivery. Even without regularly scheduled meetings, one of the clerks can be given responsibility for dropping off the completed forms at the other agency each evening on the way home.

GENERATING RESOURCES FOR COLOCATION, OUTSTATIONING, STAFF LOANS, AND JOINT INTAKE AND ASSESSMENT

Colocation, staff outstationing, staff loans, and joint intake and assessment require monetary and in-kind resources in proportion to the scope of

what is proposed. In many cases, one agency's spare room or empty desk can become another agency's outstationed staff quarters. Staff loans and temporary exchanges of staff for learning about other agencies' activities can also be carried out with minimal expense and, more important, with local decision-making authority. Thus, in many cases these coordinating activities will require little or no assistance from outside the local community. If additional support is needed, the key to success is that agencies at the local level *be committed and make known their commitment* to undertaking one or more of these approaches to coordination. Putting up in-kind resources, including the energies required to plan the effort and to think ahead to problems that might arise, is the most effective way to demonstrate to state agencies and private foundations from whom you might request assistance that you are serious and intend to go ahead.

IDEAS: Write up a brief one- to three-page description of the coordinated activity you are going to be trying at the local level. Spell out which agency is contributing space (e.g., for staff out-stationing, colocation), which is contributing clerical support (e.g., for producing the new intake and assessment forms), and so on. Send this description together with a letter requesting support (and preferably signed by all the administrators of the participating agencies) to agencies and organizations you would like to have support or become involved in the effort.

Contact the state-level representatives of the agencies that are to participate in the coordinated activity. Invite them to become involved with your local cooperative effort (e.g., send a representative to attend coordination meetings), and urge them to visit the community and see for themselves that your group is really aiming to make something happen.

Chapter 4

MUTUAL GATHERING AND USE OF INFORMATION

HOW DO YOU FIND OUT
WHAT YOU NEED TO KNOW?

Information is power! An agency that makes good use of information sources in the county and in the state or that conducts its own data collection will be better able

- to serve its clients more thoroughly by referring them to additional support services,
- to make its activities more efficient by coordinating with other agencies supplying similar or complementary services,
- to tailor its programs to the changing needs in the community,
- to write an annual report that justifies a high level of support, and
- to apply for additional funding from various sources.

Mutual information gathering, exchange, and use are the most fundamental kinds of cooperation among agencies. Without information exchange, virtually no other kind of interagency linkage is possible. On the other hand, agencies that do not coordinate their activities in any other way may still depend on each other for information—information on conditions in the community, characteristics and needs of client populations, and available services.

Some agencies broadcast the information they have available, sending newsletters or reports to many other persons and agencies in the community. Other agencies spend considerable amounts of personnel time each year searching for and accessing information, often by having their counselors contact any other organization that might have information on community needs and available services. Nevertheless, there are always many cases in which one agency needs information and another agency has the information, but the exchange is never made.

This chapter describes some of the less haphazard, more sophisticated methods of interagency collection and use of information. The first section describes how to organize and use a *centralized information clearinghouse.* The second section covers the purposes of conducting periodic *community needs assessments* and how to go about it. The final section is on *joint gathering of information about delivery of services* so as to spot frequent obstacles for clients. The checklist on the next page will help you visualize the extent to which your agency gathers and uses information in cooperation with various other types of community organizations. The blanks you do not check can suggest opportunities for you to improve the quality of interagency coordination.

ORGANIZING AN INFORMATION CLEARINGHOUSE

Recently, a survey of public and private agencies was conducted in three different communities. Agency directors were asked about their use of several classes of information related to community needs and resources: (1) population composition and mobility, (2) job-training needs, (3) job-training opportunities, (4) unemployment rates, (5) employment and economic development opportunities, (6) characteristics of persons seeking health or social services, and (7) available health, mental health, employment, or other support services. For each type of information that the agency did use, they were asked from what sources the information was accessed and how the information could be improved for the agency's purposes.

The problem mentioned most often was that each agency had to go to too many sources for the information it needed and that searching for and collecting information took a great deal of staff time each year. Many agency directors mentioned the need for a central repository or clearinghouse of information. Different agencies had different parts of the puzzle, but their similar sets of data were not in a consistent format, some being for the entire county population and others being for certain subgroups. There was agreement that a method was needed to collect and use the information cooperatively. These are the essential characteristics of an information clearinghouse.

Checklist for Mutual Gathering and Use of Information

For each set of community agencies listed below (except your own, of course), consider in what ways you cooperate with them in collecting information. *Put checks in the spaces provided to indicate if your agency has engaged in these forms of coordination in the past year.*

	Maintaining an Information Clearinghouse	*Performing a Community Needs Assessment*	*Joint Monitoring of Delivery of Services*
Employment training agencies	_____	_____	_____
Employment services offices	_____	_____	_____
Rehabilitation agencies	_____	_____	_____
Vocational education programs at:			
high schools	_____	_____	_____
colleges	_____	_____	_____
regional occupational programs or centers	_____	_____	_____
adult schools	_____	_____	_____
private vocational schools	_____	_____	_____
Health and mental health agencies	_____	_____	_____
Corrections agencies	_____	_____	_____
Economic development agencies	_____	_____	_____
Child and family services and agencies on aging	_____	_____	_____
Welfare agencies	_____	_____	_____
Community-based organizations (CBOs), community action agencies, chambers of commerce	_____	_____	_____

An Example of a Clearinghouse

In one county, a community action agency (CAA) had a large collection of curriculum materials for training. Other agencies in the community were welcome to use the materials, but almost no one knew that they existed. As part of an interagency coordination effort, the CAA staff were given the assignment of organizing the materials into a clearinghouse for use by other training providers. They entered the title, the author, and an abstract of each item into a computer file and printed out a directory with abstracts that could be searched by means of either an author index or an index of descriptor terms. The directory was sent to many public and private agencies, and now efforts are under way to expand the clearing-house. The other agencies are sending the CAA lists of materials they have that they believe would be of general interest, each with an abstract, and these are being entered into the same automated cataloging system. Soon an expanded directory will be available with each entry specifying at which agency the document can be found.

A clearinghouse can take many different forms. At the very least, agency reports and tabulations are submitted to a central location where they are organized and indexed and their availability is made known to the other agencies. After they have been cataloged, the reports and other materials may or may not be housed at a single location. A more active and responsive clearinghouse, on the other hand, might require a full-time staff person. This person's job would be (1) to compile lists of needed types of information and the times in each agency's planning cycle when they would be most useful, (2) to seek the information from local agency reports and files, from state and federal agencies, and from other sources, (3) to convert the data into the form most useful to each agency and to summarize the results, and (4) to disseminate the contents of the clearinghouse in summary reports, special tabulations for each agency, and a periodic newsletter on recent acquisitions. The right sort of clearinghouse for agencies in your community might be somewhere between.

To start up a clearinghouse, the interest and initiative of at least one agency administrator is required, and taking the lead can result in substantial benefits for the agency organizing the clearinghouse. That agency will assume a central role in the information exchange process and, because information exchange fosters other types of coordination linkages, the agency will likely become involved in joint service efforts with other providers.

Ideas for Starting a Clearinghouse

1. Hold a meeting of interested staff from several agencies to decide who will take responsibility for starting the clearinghouse, who will help get other agencies involved, and who might maintain the clearinghouse once it is started.

2. Obtain policy statements concerning client confidentiality and the confidentiality of other information on community resources (e.g., employer characteristics as reported on tax records, preliminary community improvement proposals presented by private investors to economic development centers) from each of the agencies choosing to participate in the clearinghouse. Establish procedures for the exchange of information that adhere to these confidentiality requirements (e.g., aggregating client and community resource data by categories prior to dissemination).

3. Send a checklist questionnaire to all the employment and training providers in the county, asking them (1) what information from outside their agency they would like to have available, (2) how this information would have to be aggregated or broken down to be useful, (3) when it would be needed (e.g., continually or when preparing an annual report), and (4) what reports or other information they could supply to a clearinghouse.

4. Compile the returned questionnaires into two lists: a wish-list for the clearinghouse and a list of materials that agencies could make available.

5. Match the two lists wherever possible. For items on the wish-list that no agency mentioned as being available, send a description to the agencies of the types of information that are lacking and ask them for suggestions of where the information can be found.

6. Order national and state reports that contain information useful to several agencies.

At this point, you will know the core materials needed for your clearinghouse and where they can be found. Next, you need to decide who is going to organize the clearinghouse, where the materials will be housed (at one location or at each agency), what will be done besides just cataloging the materials, and when the materials will be disseminated and updated.

PERFORMING COMMUNITY NEEDS ASSESSMENTS

A community needs assessment is a tool for documenting the gaps between current conditions in a community and required or desired conditions. These gaps, or needs, can then be ranked and the highest-priority needs selected for corrective action. For schools, juvenile corrections agencies, rehabilitation agencies, child and family service centers, and employment and training agencies, the desired goals for the community and the identified needs will naturally include obtaining career guidance, training for particular vocations, learning how to find a job and perform it adequately, and training for promotion to higher-level positions. We use these types of goals and needs to describe the needs assessment process in this section. Of course, the distinctive missions of health and human service agencies can greatly expand the scope of any community needs assessment.

The information from a needs assessment can have three major uses:

- It can be used as information for making decisions about program modifications and design of new joint programs to meet the needs of the community.

- It can be used as baseline information for (eventual) evaluation of jointly administered programs. (The design, operation, and evaluation of joint programs are discussed in Chapter 5.)

- It can be used to develop responses to program critics and detractors.

The following steps describe how to perform a thorough and rigorous needs assessment. However, you can tailor the specific activities to fit the level of interest and available resources in your agency and community. As in the case of the information exchange process, the initiative of a single agency administrator can get a needs assessment started. Once begun, the process can snowball as other agencies and the public come to understand what is being proposed. The administrator who has taken the lead can expect to be a visible force for improving community conditions.

HOW TO PERFORM A NEEDS ASSESSMENT

To be valid and useful, a needs assessment should include the views of "consumers" in determining which are the high-priority needs. The consumers of health and human service agencies include children, students, parents, older persons, employers, volunteer organizations, and community members in general. It is in the best interest of educators, local agency administrators, and the community as a whole to develop a shared responsibility for the identification of needs and the use of discretionary agency resources to meet those needs. For one thing, it will be less expensive in the long run to individual agencies if they pool their resources to survey and meet client needs. More important, joint research and action will reduce the fragmentation of the service delivery process.

A needs assessment should be a continuing process. Both economic conditions and social priorities change over time, and therefore reevaluations performed every few years are necessary to respond flexibly to changing community needs.

Summary: Community Needs Assessment

During the Needs Assessment:

1. Establish goals.
2. Rank the goals.
3. Measure the current status.
4. Develop and rank need statements.

After the Needs Assessment:

5. Organize needs by agency and program.
6. Decide how to meet needs.
7. Reassess needs.

Step 1: Establish goals. Two types of information are required for performing a needs assessment: statements of desired outcomes (goals) and indications of the current status related to those outcomes. The gaps between the two are needs. The aims of this step are to collect candidate goals from a variety of sources and to state them as clearly as possible.

Goals represent standards for performance, but there is nothing to limit agencies from going beyond these standards. The goals that are selected should make no reference to current programs or methods of implementation. Instead, goals should be stated in terms of student and client abilities and behaviors and the actions of employers, volunteer organizations, and other community groups.

The following examples of acceptable goal statements are drawn from the employment and training service area.

- Students graduating from high school will know how to apply for employment and how to interview for a job.

- A sufficient number of persons will be trained in basic accounting to meet the employment needs of businesses in the area.

- Blind and visually impaired persons will be helped to find employment commensurate with their abilities.

How are goals established? Goals can be developed by groups of educators, family counselors, health administrators, probation officers, students, and citizens who "brainstorm" about them. This might be an exercise for a career education class or an interagency workshop. Advisory committees for the community college, mental health center, employment services office, and other agencies and centers can be contacted for suggestions. *Whenever possible, consumers should be involved in the goal-setting process.*

Goals from all these sources can be collected to form a comprehensive list of desired outcomes for the community. It is particularly important that the list be comprehensive enough to represent many points of view and that the goals that are listed be clearly stated. Low-priority goals and goals with little general support can be eliminated later.

Step 2: Rank the goals. The aims of this step are to confirm the importance of the candidate goals and to rank them in order of their perceived importance. A common method of confirming the importance of proposed goals is to survey various groups of consumers requesting comments on whether or not each of the goals should be included, amended, or excluded from the needs assessment process. If many people mention a goal that was not on the list, you should seriously consider including it. If a majority of people think that a goal is inappropriate or is stated too weakly or too strongly, it can be eliminated or modified.

Whether you survey people formally or informally to confirm the importance of your goals, the next activity is a ranking exercise. You can include this as part of the same survey or do this later, when you are sure that the list of goals is complete. The results can then be combined to form an overall ranking, from the goal with the strongest support down to the goal with the least support.

Why is it necessary to rank the goals?—they may all be important. The answer is that when the goals are translated into budget commitments, decisions must be made as to where the resources are to be allocated first. As is often true in community services, everything that is needed cannot be provided.

Step 3: Measure the current status. Before the current status in the community can be measured, goal statements need to be translated into terms that can be measured, or *performance objectives.* In this step, we describe how to write performance objectives and how to go about assessing community conditions related to each objective.

For each goal, a number of performance objectives will have to be specified until there is agreement that the intent of the goal has been covered. The performance objectives might state (1) the conditions under which behaviors may be observed, (2) the minimal expectancy (that is, the percentage of a group from which certain behavior is expected or the degree of individual mastery desired), and (3) the evaluation technique to be used. Consider one of the previously described goal statements.

Goal:

A sufficient number of persons will be trained in basic accounting to meet the employment needs of businesses in the area.

Performance Objectives:

1. The number of graduates from basic accounting classes during the year will be approximately 75 percent of the projection of entry-level job openings for accountants and auditors for the year.
2. A follow-up of recent graduates from accounting courses will find that at least two-thirds are employed as accountants, auditors, purchasing agents, accounting clerks, or bookkeepers six months after leaving school.
3. In a survey of businesses, employers will rarely list entry-level accountants or auditors as job openings they had trouble filling.

Next, methods must be found to assess the community's current status with respect to each performance objective. Information can be collected from agencies' annual reports and other periodic summaries of administrative data, from the records of samples of students, from a survey of clients or businesses, or from any other source appropriate to the performance objective. With careful organization, all the performance objectives that require a survey of one community group, say employers, can be measured at the same time, as can all the objectives that require a survey of past clients, and so on.

Performance Objective:

In a survey of businesses, employers will rarely list entry-level accountants or auditors as job openings they had trouble filling.

Item on a Survey of Employers:

For each of the following types of job positions, please indicate how many entry-level job openings of that type your business had during the year and how many of those you had trouble filling (i.e., the position remained vacant for two months or more):

Type of Position	Number of Entry-Level Openings Last Year	Number You Had Trouble Filling
Purchasing agent	_____	_____
Auditor	_____	_____
Accounting clerk	_____	_____
Bookkeeper	_____	_____
Payroll/timekeeping clerk	_____	_____

Lack of a ready-made test or measurement method does not change the fundamental importance of a goal and its performance objectives. Instead, creative thought should be put to the problem of how some data about the performance objectives can be gathered, even if indirectly.

Step 4: Develop and rank need statements. Statements about the gaps between the desired and actual status in the community on particular performance objectives are need statements. Need statements are listed without reference to the causes or reasons for the gaps or what might be done to reduce them. They are simple statements of fact, and the aims of this step are to develop, rank, and disseminate these statements.

Examples of Need Statements

1. Fifty-two students graduated from basic accounting classes in the past year. Seventy-five percent of the projection of entry-level job openings in accounting in the county is only 27. Approximately 25 too many accounting students were trained.
2. A survey of graduates from accounting courses the previous year found only one-third employed in accounting or related occupations. Since the performance objective stated that two-thirds of the graduates should have found such employment, approximately one-third too few were able to find jobs related to their training.
3. In a survey of the 100 largest businesses in the county, only 3 reported having difficulty filling an entry-level job opening in accounting or auditing. This means that the performance objective has been met.

When performance objectives are compared to measures of current status and need statements are written, these statements can be grouped according to the general goals from which they were derived. Since the goals have already been ranked (in Step 2), *it is now possible to tell which groups of needs are most critical, based on their position in the list.* A master list of community needs can now be disseminated to all interested parties. The gaps can be displayed graphically, and explanations of terms can be given if the vocabulary is not likely to be familiar to all readers. The process by which the needs statements were identified should be described fully. At this point the needs assessment is done, but there are several important steps to be taken after the needs assessment if all this thinking and ranking and investigating is to be worth the time and effort.

WHAT TO DO AFTER A NEEDS ASSESSMENT

Step 5: Organize needs by agency and program. The next step is to construct a matrix of the critical needs that have been identified by all the major health and human service agencies and programs in the community. After you have indicated which agencies now have programs for reducing which needs, you will probably find that, in many cases, none of the agencies has any programs related to particular needs. Gaps in student performance, client health or welfare, or employee availability are often the result of gaps in the public and private service systems. Not all needs will be so simply understood, however. The reasons for some gaps in performance may be complex and interrelated with general societal problems.

Step 6: Decide how to meet needs. So far, you will have identified needs in the community and the location of current programs for address-ing those needs. However, unless the needs assessment leads to an attempt to improve the performance of the system, it will largely have been a waste of time and effort. The next step is to meet with staff from the various agencies to attempt to discover the reasons for the existence of gaps in performance. Work groups may be established within individual agencies, or they may address general concerns and be made up of staff from several agencies. These groups will have to consider carefully various causes that are suggested, and brainstorming sessions might be held to list all the possible ways the causes could be eliminated and the needs reduced.

Some needs can be met by individual agencies working alone. In most cases, however, the solution will require two or more agencies jointly designing and implementing a program (or a modification of an existing program) to deal with the problem.

Step 7: Reassess needs. After an agreed-upon period of time, the programs designed to reduce needs in the community can be evaluated. Evaluation information can then be used to refine the program while it is

in the process of reducing the need (that is, to reassess the decisions and plans made under Step 6). Has the need been met? If not, then more meetings should be held to modify the program or to design new approaches.

Now that you have read through the details of the process, you might want to go back to the list of steps at the beginning of this section and consider what needs assessment activities would be appropriate for your community.

GATHERING INFORMATION ABOUT
DELIVERY OF SERVICES

This last form of joint information collection and analysis complements the information supplied by a community needs assessment. Community needs are identified with respect to *outcomes* (goals and performance objectives). In contrast, information about delivery of services is used to find problems related to *processes:* unnecessary duplication in the activities performed by staff in various agencies and frequent problems in processing and referring clients or operating service programs.

Not all duplication between agencies is undesirable. It is sometimes desirable to have job-search workshops presented at more than one agency, for example, or to have family counseling services available at several locations. Frequently, however, agencies try to supply a range of services much wider than their primary responsibility, and staff time spent on these "auxiliary" services can detract from the quality of the core services of that particular agency. In these cases, returning to a bit more specialization of function among schools, service agencies, and human development centers can result in greater efficiency and higher quality of services.

Agency administrators are sometimes too busy with budgetary and management concerns to be fully aware of the problems that clients with particular ability levels or needs or in particular circumstances can often pose for their staff. Even more frequently, administrators may not know what problems their operating procedures are causing students or other clients. Although some of these problems can be adequately dealt with by one agency working alone, others require an interagency response to deal with the problem completely and effectively. For example, serving certain clients adequately may require that training and support services from more than one agency by arranged for and delivered. One agency can attempt to improve its efforts to make such arrangements. However, a multiagency approach will be necessary to ensure smooth service delivery to persons in need. The administrator who recognizes this interdependence at the earliest point and decides to make the best of it will gain the appreciation of his or her agency's clients and the respect of the agency's staff.

The easiest way of gathering information about delivery of services is to question the staff persons who work directly with clients. (You might want to consider also a survey of students or clients to get their perspective on the services provided.) Some example questions follow. A short questionnaire can easily be put together and circulated, and the returned answers can be tabulated and used in agency planning. For example, the results of such a survey can be summarized to show the average time spent by staff on various activities that are not the primary mission of the agency and to present categories of problems frequently encountered by the agency and its clients during the delivery of services.

A single agency or school could choose to survey its staff and analyze the results in isolation. There are major benefits, however, from having several agencies that frequently interact survey their staffs simultaneously. Following the survey, these agencies can meet to discuss the results and explore joint solutions to some of the problems uncovered. The issue of how much duplication of functions is desirable among agencies and whether some redundancy should be eliminated by having selected agencies perform those functions can only be addressed in a meeting of agency administrators. Similarly, some process-related problems for staff and for clients require an interagency solution. In addition, staff suggestions for improving the relations and coordination among agencies are quite likely to lead to improved procedures. As is so often true, *dealing with problems from several perspectives at once results in more comprehensive and workable solutions.*

Questions for Staff about Delivery of Services

1. Describe your principal work responsibilities.

2. How many hours per week on the average do you spend on the following activities (whether or not they are part of your principal work responsibilities)?

   _____ Administering interest inventories, ability tests, or other assessment instruments

   _____ Giving personal or vocational counseling

   _____ Teaching classes

   _____ Conducting workshops for clients (e.g., on how to stay within a family budget or how to find a job)

   _____ Finding jobs or housing for clients

   _____ Finding health or financial services for persons in need

3. Do any of these activities interfere with your primary duties? If so, please explain.

4. Describe one or two recent incidents where the abilities, needs, or circumstances of a client (or student) caused some problems for you. (No names, please.)

5. Describe one or two recent incidents from your experience where the way we operate our program caused some problems or inconveniences for one or more clients (or students), or where they were dissatisfied with the training or services they received.

6. In what ways could our relations with other agencies in the county be improved, either to supply better or more comprehensive services or to make our operation more efficient?

Chapter 5

INTEGRATED PROGRAM ADMINISTRATION

WHAT DO YOU DO WHEN
COORDINATION OF EXISTING PROGRAMS
IS NOT ENOUGH?

Integrating the services of several agencies for the purpose of meeting community needs more effectively requires joint program *design, operation,* and *evaluation.* Whether this integration represents an entirely new service delivery approach (such as a demonstration) or just a changed configuration of existing services, the participants will have to come to grips with these three main components of shared administrative responsibility.

Design, operation, and evaluation are separate but interrelated phases in the development of a new service delivery program. Design decisions directly affect what is evaluated, and evaluation activities and their results lead to further refinements in design. The diagram below illustrates the interrelationships among these three components of program administration.

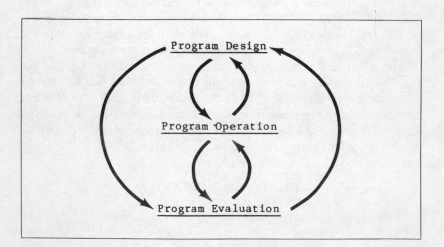

JOINT PROGRAM DESIGN

Because the idea for an integrated approach will often occur to one member of a planning group initially, the task for this individual is to present his or her idea to the others in such a way as to catch their interest and, eventually, secure their commitment. At this early stage, it is not important to spell out all the details of the original idea. It is better to work with a more general description of both the need to be served and the approach to be taken. It *is* important, however, to put the idea on paper. In this way, other agency representatives have some*thing* to react to and carry away with them to their own offices for further study and written comment.

When the planning group has achieved some consensus on the extent of need and the type of program that is required, it is time for one or more members of the group to take responsibility for preparing a detailed description of what the integrated program will look like. A good first step in this process is to develop a *systems analysis* of the program, which describes the logic of how the program will operate to achieve its goals. When the systems analysis is reviewed by the group and revised into final form, it is ready to be presented to the policy boards of the agencies that are to participate in operating the program. A systems analysis is an especially effective tool for communicating service proposals to policy-making bodies, because it is succinct yet detailed and demonstrates that considerable thought has gone into the planning and design phases.

The detail of such a comprehensive program description is also invaluable to the planning group of agency administrators, since it clearly sets out individual agency responsibilities as well as an action plan for achieving desired goals. (In this sense, a systems analysis serves a purpose that is similar to that of the memorandum of agreement discussed in Chapter 2.). The systems analysis also points out the responsibilities expected of staff in the participating agencies. It is critical that these staff, who may not have been involved in the development of the program plan, be provided with the necessary orientation to ease the transition from the current to the new procedure. (See the orientation tips on page 90.)

JOINT PROGRAM OPERATION

As the program design is translated into action and the needs for certain refinements are met, agency representatives must work out procedures to manage program activities, budgetary needs, and technical assistance

Developing a Systems Analysis

To prepare an analysis of how a planned service delivery approach will work, it is necessary (1) to organize the intended outcomes from the most specific objectives to the most far-reaching goals, (2) to identify the various phases of program operation and the key activities associated with each phase, and (3) to anticipate conditions in the agencies or in the community that are outside the direct control of the program but can either help or hurt program operation. When these tasks are accomplished, it is possible to diagram how the program will work, beginning with the earliest *inputs* (e.g., staff, facilities), continuing with the *processes* that follow from these inputs (e.g., performance of client screening activities), and ending up with the *outcomes* that are to be achieved as a result of these processes (e.g., clients placed in training programs or referred for additional counseling). The outline for a systems analysis would generally follow the simple format given below, but with much more detail.

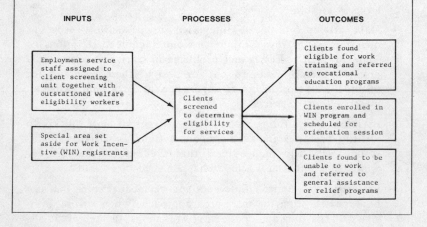

requirements. While a single agency can take the lead in dealing with these matters, using the other agency representatives on the joint planning body as "program advisers," it is preferable for an integrated approach to be followed throughout the course of program development. The apparent efficiency of a single agency assuming all management responsibilities is usually overrated and may lead to the waning of interest in the program by other administrators and their policy boards.

Orienting Staff to the Integrated Program

- Prepare a written overview of the purpose of the integrated program that highlights the contributions to be made by the various work groups. Pay particular attention to how these groups will be expected to coordinate their activities with other staff to accomplish program objectives.

- Conduct workshops with all the staff who are to perform similar functions in the program (e.g., client screening). Prepare handouts that summarize the tasks they will be expected to carry out and that they can use as reminders for the first few days on the job.

- Be prepared in these initial discussions with staff to answer their questions concerning any changes in their employment status as a result of being assigned to an integrated effort. For example, the seniority systems of public agencies may appear to be affected when staff from different agencies are assigned to do the same jobs as part of an integrated service delivery program. In particular, staff who are to be retrained to perform new jobs will want to know whether there will be any change in their titles or job levels as a result.

- Make attempts to locate integrated service delivery programs operating in nearby communities and include descriptions of some of their successes and problems in staff presentations. If possible, arrange visits to one or two of these programs for selected staff so they can experience at first hand what an integrated system is like.

- Establish a monitoring system that will permit staff quickly to identify problems and take remedial actions. Description of this system will help reduce fears that the new service delivery approach is a disaster waiting to happen.

- Emphasize the positive outcomes and personal rewards that can be expected from the integrated approach. When writing overviews of the program, conducting workshops, or holding discussions with program staff, be sure to note how the work routine will become more efficient and that a greater proportion of staff time will be freed to be spent in helping clients rather than handling administrative obstacles. Of course, emphasizing the positive is no substitute for strong administrative and policy board support, and the strength of these commitments to the program must be clearly communicated to all staff members.

Sharing Management Responsibilities

- To foster a sense of group ownership of a program, the planning group can hire a program director to manage day-to-day activities who is not designated administratively as an employee of any of the agencies involved. Although he or she may interact with individual agency representatives, the director serves as an employee of the planning group and therefore reports to all the members.

- Different representatives on the planning group may want to assume primary responsibilities for their components of the integrated program. For example, the employment service representative could take charge of job search activities, educational agency representatives might assume responsibility for directing the vocational assessment portions of the program, and economic development centers could play the lead role in encouraging participation of the private sector in creating work activities. This approach has often been successful, but care must be taken to ensure that planning meetings focus on the total effort, not just on one or two program components. It is easy to revert to the "go-it-alone" approach, and, for this reason, participating administrators must try to be sensitive and respond quickly to any budding turfsmanship.

- Establishing management teams at both supervisorial and staff levels is also a good approach for sharing program responsibilities. Team meetings can be scheduled to take place weekly or biweekly for the first several months and then changed to a less demanding schedule.

In one county, a council of top-level agency administrators designed an ambitious integrated program to serve employment training agency clients and persons needing welfare assistance. The participating agencies and their roles are described in the next box. At the center of this diagram, the County Coordinated Planning Council is designated as the formal administrative body for the program, with the policy boards of the participating agencies serving as the final boards of review for program design decisions. Representatives from each participating agency are in charge of their own program segments, and the monthly council meetings are used to assess how well the various components are operating and coordinating with one another. Plans have been made to establish management teams at various staff levels. Because this program was in operation when an increase occurred recently in the county in the numbers of refugees seeking services, over 2300 of these new (and unexpected!) clients were served without delay. This is an example of the power of an integrated service system.

SHARING BUDGETARY RESPONSIBILITIES

Unlike the sharing of program management responsibilities, which may be approached using a variety of interagency strategies, joint budgeting procedures will often be dictated by the types of funding sources that are tapped. If a grant is received from a state agency or a private foundation, for example, it may be necessary for a single agency to serve as the primary fiscal agent, although all participating agencies may be involved in decisions affecting resources allocation. When the funds for program operation are received piecemeal, with each agency supporting its own program segment, integrated budgeting may be limited to joint decision making regarding the allocation of resources. In contrast, *the greatest potential for exploring more creative approaches to sharing budgetary responsibilities lies with the administration of program resources that are generated locally*—in-kind contributions, volunteer support, and private donations. Because these resources belong to the program, interagency approaches to budget administration, cost accounting, and projections of resource needs and availability can be tried. When funds for the program become a shared responsibility, standardized forms and uniform record-keeping procedures for monitoring program resources can be designed and put to use.

It is important that the accounting sections from different agencies be involved in discussions concerning the integrated program at an early

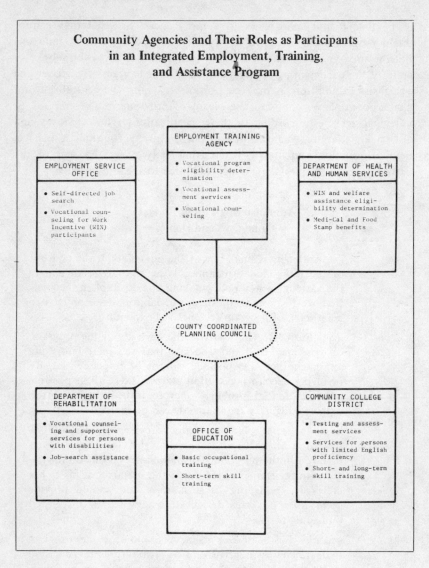

Community Agencies and Their Roles as Participants in an Integrated Employment, Training, and Assistance Program

EMPLOYMENT TRAINING AGENCY

- Vocational program eligibility determination
- Vocational assessment services
- Vocational counseling

EMPLOYMENT SERVICE OFFICE

- Self-directed job search
- Vocational counseling for Work Incentive (WIN) participants

DEPARTMENT OF HEALTH AND HUMAN SERVICES

- WIN and welfare assistance eligibility determination
- Medi-Cal and Food Stamp benefits

COUNTY COORDINATED PLANNING COUNCIL

DEPARTMENT OF REHABILITATION

- Vocational counseling and supportive services for persons with disabilities
- Job-search assistance

OFFICE OF EDUCATION

- Basic occupational training
- Short-term skill training

COMMUNITY COLLEGE DISTRICT

- Testing and assessment services
- Services for persons with limited English proficiency
- Short- and long-term skill training

point. In addition to making clear what (individual agency) budgetary constraints the program will have to live with, these business office representatives can begin to work on identifying ways of cross-referencing required budget tasks and establishing a language for cost-accounting procedures that is understandable to all parties and to the administrators at the federal and state levels. If some agencies feel that they cannot obtain waivers from having to keep their own budget records, point out that the fiscal management of the joint program will always be subject to audit by the participating agencies and by their federal or state accounting specialists. In addition, it may be possible to equip the centralized program-accounting system with the means of providing budget reports to individual agencies according to their specifications. The efficiency and cost savings that are usually realized from a central accounting or management information system will often completely cover the cost of the software needed for producing budgets tailored to specific formats.

Administering a Joint Budget: Some Do's and Don'ts

Do: inform business managers at the outset about the concept of the integrated program and the support for it among the various agency policymaking bodies. Explain the goals that are to be accomplished, and ask for advice on how to keep track of program receipts and expenditures.

Don't: leave business office staff in the dark about the program, or you may find out too late that the joint budgeting approach that was planned cannot be implemented. By involving accounting section staff at the earliest possible point, potential problems due to inflexibility in interpreting budgetary requirements can be avoided.

Do: have the joint planning council review various budget-related forms currently being used by the agencies involved in the program. This familiarizes each administrator with the frames of reference and practices of his or her colleagues regarding fiscal matters and should provide good ideas for the design of a new set of integrated budgeting forms.

Don't: use the forms of one agency to monitor the program budget. This agency is likely to misinterpret this decision and to regard itself as the primary fiscal agent and decision maker for the program.

Do: have program supervisors or management teams project what their resource needs will be several months ahead. The planning council can then review these estimates, suggest changes if necessary, and keep track of expenditures made in relation to these estimates. Management teams should also have the opportunity to know where they stand relative to their projections and to revise their projections for the next month or so in light of actual expenditures and changing demands.

Don't: commit the program to the pattern and rate of expenditures stated in the initial program design, or allow planning council members to take sole responsibility for monitoring the program budget. This approach is too inflexible (i.e., it allows for no learning based on experience) and will cause staff working on the program to pay little attention to reports of program expenditures.

PROVIDING STAFF SUPPORT

There is no more important component for ensuring both the immediate success and the longer-term impacts of an integrated services program than providing the staff working in the program with *constructive* assistance on a timely basis. Working at new tasks and working with new people in new surroundings may cause even the most reliable staff persons to become a bit uncertain of their abilities and work roles. Performance standards, employee comparisons, and program evaluations that are used to penalize staff can ensure failure. In contrast, technical assistance, workshops and consultants, and program evaluation results that suggest useful program modifications can help to prevent minor difficulties from growing into insurmountable problems.

IDEA: Have planning council members meet on a regular basis with program management teams and with individual staff members to understand how these individuals perceive their own contributions to the success of the program. Ask program staff for suggestions of ways to improve the work environment and overall program performance. (Reread the example questions on improving the service delivery system presented near the end of Chapter 4 for suggestions of how to go about surveying program staff about their work activities.)

While it is impossible to list all the signs that indicate program staff are in need of assistance, some indications are typical, and keeping an eye out for them can be useful. They often emerge in the expression of attitudes. The checklist below presents some of these attitudes together with responses that have proven successful in resolving the underlying problems.

Diagnosing and Meeting Staff Needs

Attitudinal Warning Signs	*Constructive Responses*
1. "I don't want to give up the work responsibilities I'm good at."	Point out that job skills are learned and that acquiring new skills will enhance future job opportunities. Let the staff person know that you think he or she *can* learn the new skills and, in your opinion, it must be tried.
2. "I'm afraid that adapting to a new work role will be too difficult."	Explain that you expect the change process to be a gradual one, with all staff learning new skills and accepting new responsibilities gradually. Note that, after all, you're all really learning together to make the program work.
3. "The present methods for helping clients seem to be good enough."	Agree that the present situation is acceptable but that there is a need to be even more effective in meeting client needs with existing resources. Stress that this is really a necessity, given

the present concerns over agency spending and the prospects of reduced budgets.

4. "Changing to a new service approach will make people think that what we've been doing for years wasn't effective." Suggest that it is important to make changes when they are warranted by new knowledge concerning service delivery processes and the prospects of reduced funding. Reassure the individual that changes will be made gradually, so that everyone (including clients) will become comfortable with them.

JOINT PROGRAM EVALUATION

The systems analysis, which describes how the program was intended to accomplish its objectives, serves as a basic element in the program evaluation and improvement process. Questions about the effectiveness of particular program activities follow directly from the detailed description provided by the systems analysis. In this way, *the systems analysis of the program that was put together during the design phase serves as a road map for the evaluation.*

Given the need to put evaluation resources to work effectively, the first task must be to limit the questions to be studied to the ones that are most important for future decisions. It is usually impractical (and too expensive!) to address *all* the issues in a single evaluation study, so a method is required for analyzing which information will best serve the decision-making responsibilities of the interagency council overseeing the program. One approach to carrying out a *decision analysis* as part of preparing a program evaluation is described in the next box.

Analyzing Decision Requirements

Different lines of reasoning can lead to different decisions. Identifying the information needed to support or reject particular lines of reasoning allows evaluation results to be linked directly to decision making.

To begin this type of analysis, each member of the joint planning council can be interviewed concerning the program-related decisions he or she will be considering based on the evaluation results. Let's look at an example of how the analysis of one decision, *whether or not to expand the scope of an integrated program to serve unskilled, delinquent youths,* can lead to clear-cut direction for the evaluation. Possible reasons for this decision include:

1. finding that these youths are receiving more comprehensive and appropriate assistance than they would have without this interagency cooperation;
2. finding that the staffs of the department of corrections and other local agencies are developing additional capabilities because of the interagency contacts; and
3. finding that the integrated service delivery approach can be more cost-effective in meeting the needs of unskilled, delinquent youths.

If these were the most prominent reasons for making that decision, then the information needed from the evaluation to support or reject these reasons would be:

1. descriptions of how the integrated program has affected the comprehensiveness and appropriateness of assistance received by these youths;
2. descriptions of knowledge and capabilities developed by agency staff through the interagency contacts and an assessment of the usefulness of those skills for assisting this youth population; and
3. information concerning the cost-effectiveness of the integrated program compared to the past performance of the constituent agencies.

DEVELOPING EVALUATION INDICATORS

To select the specific information items, or indicators, for the evaluation, it is best to start with a clear understanding of what you want to measure (the variables) and then to make explicit the reason for asserting *this* indicator is a measure of *that* variable. For example, if you want to measure whether minority youth are receiving more comprehensive and appropriate assistance and think that an indicator of this might be the extent to which agency services are accessible to this client group, it is a good idea to state *why* this seems an appropriate indicator. (In this case, the reason might be that before services can be comprehensive and appropriate, they must be accessible.) By clearly stating your reasons for selecting particular indicators, colleagues in other agencies helping with the evaluation will be better able to understand how the indicators relate to decision-making needs and will be able to offer constructive comments. Moreover, the interagency planning council will have an easier time understanding what the evaluation results mean if the relationships of particular indicators to decisions regarding program performance are known in advance.

When the evaluation indicators are being decided upon, it is necessary to determine which indicators can be measured using existing data (for example, from agency records) and which will require that new data (for instance, from interviews of program staff or clients) be collected. Scarce resources favor the use of existing data. The particular information needs of decision makers, however, may not be satisfied by data that have been collected for other purposes. They may want to know, for example, whether unskilled, delinquent youths perceive that the services available to them are sufficient to meet their needs. For this reason, surveys conducted on a limited scale may be required in addition to existing data sources. Many different types of existing and new data sources have been used to evaluate cooperative agency efforts in the past. A representative selection of these data sources is presented in the next box, together with the variables and indicators they were used to assess.

VARIABLES	INDICATORS	DATA SOURCES
Agencies formulate approaches for integrating services	Number of contacts between agency administrators and policy boards to formulate approaches	Individuals' appointment books or calendars, advisory board agendas and minutes
	Number and type of service approaches proposed	Agency working documents, directed observations
	Number and type of cooperative planning activities designed on the basis of proposed approaches	Agency working documents, interviews
Approaches for integrating services implemented	(Example) Welfare Department staff loaned to Employment Services Office to provide support services counseling	Agency records and reports, directed observations
	(Example) Unskilled, delinquent youth enroll in new courses at the community college, adult school, or regional occupational program	Agency records and reports
	(Example) Mental Health Center services linked with training services components of the Department of Rehabilitation and the community college	Local newspapers and newsletters, agency records
Support of private industry	Number of private groups taking steps to learn more about the services and needs of the integrated efforts	Local newspapers, radio/TV broadcasts, industry reports

	Number of private groups expressing public approval or support for these efforts	Local newspapers, agency memoranda
	Number of private groups organizing themselves to work with these efforts	Industry newsletters, minutes of advisory group meetings, radio/TV broadcasts
	Amount and types of resources provided by private groups to underwrite program costs	Local newspapers, interviews, industry newsletters
Employment assistance accelerated	Number and types of employment-related services provided to clients not served in the past	Case files, surveys of agencies
	Number of persons receiving complementary services from two or more agencies simultaneously	Agency records, case files
	Costs to employment training and education agencies of providing occupational skills training	Agency expenditure reports
	Range of occupational skills training alternatives available to clients	Course catalogues, agency bulletins and newsletters
	Increased participation and linkage of private sector in placement of clients	Interviews, surveys of local employers

DESIGNING THE EVALUATION

An evaluation design is a plan describing how information is to be collected for assessing the evaluation indicators. The complexity of the design will depend on the questions to be answered (from the decision analysis), the level of certainty desired in identifying and attributing effects to the program, and the resources that are available for the evaluation. Many textbooks have been written that deal exclusively with the topic of evaluation design. In this section, only two major issues that affect the choice of a design are discussed: *validity* and *frame of reference*. Validity has to do with whether the evaluation assesses what it was intended to assess. Frame of reference describes the point of view taken by the evaluators in assessing program operations. Let's take a closer look at each of these evaluation design considerations.

NOTE: If you are considering spending a fair portion of your interagency budget on conducting what you hope will be a definitive evaluation of your program, our best advice is to supplement this introduction with the easy-to-read, surprisingly comprehensive, and useful reference guide written by Carol Weiss:

Weiss, Carol H. *Evaluation research: Methods of assessing program effectiveness.* Englewood Cliffs, NJ: Prentice-Hall, 1972.
A revised and updated Second Edition of Peter H. Rossi and Howard E. Freeman's *Evaluation: A Systematic Approach,* which features seventy-five illustrative case modules ("exhibits") is also available.

Rossi, Peter H., & Freeman, Howard E. *Evaluation: A systematic approach* (2nd ed.). Beverly Hills, CA: Sage Publications, 1982.

Validity can be broken down into two components: *internal validity* and *external validity*. Both of these are important to consider when an evaluation design is selected.

- An evaluation is *internally valid* if the answers produced by the evaluation take into account all important aspects of program operation and are not affected by the methods used to collect information. To ensure high internal validity, all important data identified by the systems analysis of the program should be collected. In addition, care must be taken that the data-collection methods do not alter the facts (an example would be interviewing clients about their opinions of an agency while they are applying for services from that agency).

- An evaluation is *externally valid* if the answers produced by the evaluation can be applied in new situations (for example, in starting up a new integrated services project). To ensure high external validity, it is necessary to make sure there is nothing particularly "special" about the agencies, staff persons, or clients participating in the program being evaluated. Another way of saying this is that the components of the program and the people involved should be representative, or typical, of the types of facilities and personnel that would be encountered in other settings.

Evaluations always involve comparisons, and it is essential that the interagency group overseeing the integrated program be clear about the *frame of reference* they wish to apply in judging the program's effectiveness. The frame of reference for an evaluation determines the type of comparisons to be made.

Relative vs. Absolute Comparisons

Relative comparisons are comparisons to what would have occurred without the program or to other types of programs for accomplishing similar objectives. For example, if your group wants to know whether the integrated services approach is more effective than what was done by individual agencies in the past, the costs and benefits of the program must be compared to the estimated costs and benefits of previous efforts.

Absolute comparisons are comparisons to particular desired outcomes. For example, a training program's expenditures could be compared to the goal of keeping costs under $100 per participant. The important element here is to gain agreement on the criteria, or goals, by which the program is to be evaluated. This emphasizes the importance of the program design phase, when the desired objectives and longer-term impacts of the program were conceptualized.

PUTTING EVALUATION RESULTS TO WORK

The systems analysis of the program, which guides the selection of evaluation indicators, is the key to turning evaluation findings into program improvements. At one level, indicators of the availability of certain inputs (such as staff) or the occurrence or timing of specific processes (such as client screening procedures) may point out aspects of the program in need of refinement. For example, the finding that too few eligibility workers actually were assigned to the program might result in the decision to reassign staff on a part-time basis from other program areas to help out. Similarly, the finding that the lengthy time requirements of screening clients were causing delays in the start-up of training programs might lead designers to restructure the screening component or to reschedule the vocational or life-skills classes.

At a more significant level, "why" questions based on the systems analysis can lead to answers that may change the overall program design. For example, if the inputs and processes believed to be necessary for the achievement of a specific objective occurred but the objective itself did not, the answer to the accompanying "why not?" may force the planning group back to the drawing board. What factors were not accounted for? Was the reluctance of non-English-speaking persons to seek assistance from public agencies underestimated? Should a public relations effort to attract these persons be made a part of the integrated program? Could the approach to assessing job skills be handled differently, so that employers would play a greater role in meeting with and screening applicants? Answers to these types of questions can be expected to alter the program design and set the stage for further evaluation at a later time.

In the same way the systems analysis of the program helps to put evaluation results to work in improving program performance, the analysis of decisions can be used to guide the dissemination of evaluation results. Because the interagency council sponsoring the integrated program is the major stakeholders' group for the evaluation (that is, those persons with a "stake" in the program's performance and success), findings from the evaluation can be tied directly to their decision-making needs. Whether

results are presented to these agency representatives orally or in written form, it is useful to review the decisions that provided focus for the evaluation and indicate the extent to which the findings support or do not support particular decisions.

Identifying and Informing Stakeholder Groups

In addition to the interagency group administering the integrated services program, be sure to identify other potentially important audiences. After conferring with other agency representatives to determine which persons, agencies, and advisory councils should be informed of the program's performance, try in your reports to make these audiences "stakeholders after the fact."

- Find out what decisions they will be making that concern local-level coordination among health and human service organizations.

- Make up a schedule of their decision-making deadlines or planning cycles so that you can have your evaluation reports prepared when they will be most useful.

- Decide on the findings to present to each group by considering (1) their decision-making needs, (2) the level of detail they are likely to require, and (3) the types of comparisons that would be most effective in informing them of your program's accomplishments.

- Tie the findings you present *directly* to the matters of greatest concern to these groups.

- Select reporting formats carefully so that each group receives the type of report it will read. For some audiences, for example, charts and graphs will be best, while for others, a brief overview written in a narrative style will be more effective.

AFTERWORD

Themes that influence federal legislation, state policymaking, and local practice take time to become prominent. They may first appear in a single community, spreading outward and upward over a period of several years. Alternatively, ideas that arise at federal and state levels may trickle down to counties and cities slowly, through new mandates, technical assistance opportunities, and funds for innovative projects. The concept of inter-agency coordination to serve clients better is one theme whose history has known both of these bottom-up and top-down origins.

When we began to gather material for this guide in 1979, there clearly was a growing feeling among federal and state agencies that local-level coordination was important. Twenty years of research on the subject, the accomplishments of special projects, and the frustrations associated with unnecessary duplications in the service delivery system had created a favorable climate for emphasizing interagency planning and program integration. During the course of our work, the realities of sharp budget reductions caused the climate to become even more propitious.

At the present time, interagency coordination is viewed by many persons at federal, state, and local levels as perhaps the best hope for preserving the quality of services to clients. We concur in this view and have, as a result, special interest that this guide be used effectively by local service providers. In this closing section, we would like to suggest some ways the book could be used in your organization. As you find other uses for it, don't forget to share your insights with your colleagues in other agencies.

MAKING THE GUIDE WORK FOR YOU

* Provide local agencies and branch offices with sufficient copies so that staff will be able to browse through the guide when they have free

time. Keep one or two copies available at the offices for use by staff while at work.

• Make copies of the various quizzes that appear in the handbook and ask staff to spend a few moments filling them out. Use these quizzes as ways of generating interest in the topics presented.

• Have different staff take the lead in reading through a chapter and organizing informal (say, lunchtime) discussion groups to consider main topics. To stimulate interest, suggest the names of persons in the community who might be called upon to talk about some of the themes—a great opportunity for bringing in staff from other agencies!

• Personally take charge of improving some aspect of coordination between your agency and others. If you don't take the responsibility for starting, who will? By assuming the lead, you will be in a position to see some of your ideas turned into accomplishments, and your initiative will probably not go unnoticed!

GLOSSARY

Absolute Comparison—Comparison of program performance to particular desired outcomes (e.g., goals). (page 103)

Case Consultation—Staff at one agency ask advice from staff at another agency regarding the needs of particular clients. (page 55)

Case Management—Staff at one agency are given responsibility for coordinating the services provided by several agencies to meet the needs of particular clients. (page 58)

Client Conference—Staff from two or more agencies discuss the needs of clients they have in common informally and as needed. (page 55)

Client Team—Staff from two or more agencies coordinate services to meet the needs of mutual clients through continuous and systematic interaction. (page 56)

Colocation—Two or more agencies have staff and separate facilities at the same location—coordination of activities is optional. (page 61)

Crisis Operation—The "putting out fires" mode in which many agencies operate, which can serve as an obstacle to cooperative efforts with other agencies. (page 38)

Cross-Referral Network—Two or more agencies regularly refer clients back and forth, keeping track of their capabilities for providing services and monitoring the effectiveness of the referral process in meeting client needs. (page 52)

Decision Analysis—A method for identifying the information required in decision making. (page 97)

Economies of Scale—The cost-per-client savings that often accrue when the one agency best able to perform a service does it for the clients of all agencies. (page 13)

External Validity—The extent to which evaluation results in certain situations can be accurately generalized, or applied, to other situations. (page 102)

Fragmentation of Services—Lack of planning about the full range of services that a client may need and lack of coordination of services that are provided by different agencies. (page 53)

Goals—Broad, general statements of agency or program intent, as contrasted with more precise, measurable performance objectives. (page 78)

Information Clearinghouse—Staff at one location have responsibility for collection, classification, and distribution of information to several agencies, such as on housing conditions, job openings, and client services available. (page 72)

Internal Validity—The extent to which an evaluation produces accurate results concerning program performance. (page 102)

Joint Intake and Assessment—Two or more agencies develop a common system of processing new clients and diagnosing their needs to coordinate and improve the delivery of services from all relevant agencies. (page 67)

Joint Program Design—Two or more agencies unite their efforts to plan and find resources for a joint project. (page 88)

Joint Program Evaluation—Two or more agencies unite their efforts to assess the effectiveness of a joint project. (page 97)

Joint Program Operation—Two or more agencies unite their efforts in the implementation of a program. (page 88)

Linkage—Any ongoing relationship or interaction between two agencies, whether formalized or the result of an informal agreement. (page 46)

Memorandum of Agreement—A nonfinancial and nonbinding agreement between two or more agencies specifying a set of common objectives and describing the roles and responsibilities of each agency. (page 44)

Needs Assessment—The gathering and analysis of information on community needs. (page 76)

Need Statements—Statements about the gaps between the desired and actual status in the community on particular performance objectives. (page 82)

Performance Objectives—The specific, measurable outcomes intended by a program or agency, which make the more global goals concrete and meaningful. (page 80)

Protection of Investment—The benefit obtained when certain programs make other programs more useful and effective, as job placement programs do for job-training programs. (page 54)

Referral—Staff at one agency advise persons with needs to seek services at another agency. (page 49)

Relative Comparison—Comparison of program performance to what would have occurred without the program or to other types of programs seeking to accomplish similar objectives. (page 103)

Resources Assessment—The gathering and analysis of information on program or agency resources, often with respect to their availability for some new or joint effort. (page 18)

Reward Structures—Official and unofficial rules specifying which activities are disapproved of and which activities are rewarded. Examples include job descriptions, promotion criteria, agency funding formulas based on caseloads, and the ways in which numbers of clients served are counted. (page 19)

Staff Outstationing—Staff from one agency are assigned to do their work in the facilities of another agency—coordination is necessary. (page 63)

Staff Loan—Staff from one agency are assigned to work (temporarily) under the direct supervision of another agency to carry out activities for that agency. (page 64)

Systems Analysis—A diagram that describes the intended sequence of activities by which a program will achieve its goals. (page 88)

Turfsmanship—Attempts to extend individual agency responsibilities and clients and resist cooperation, caused in large part by the absence of cooperative reward structures. (page 39)

Uniform Record-Keeping—Two or more agencies use standardized forms (such as client application forms) so that clients need not fill out similar forms at each agency and so that information can be exchanged in comparable form among agencies. (page 92)

ANNOTATED BIBLIOGRAPHY

The reference materials annotated in this section are useful supplements to the present guide. Each annotation describes the contents of the material and relates it to specific topics and themes presented in this volume. To enable readers to obtain these reports and books, the order numbers assigned by centralized information clearinghouses and the addresses of publishers are provided.

For materials available from the National Technical Information Service (NTIS), paper copies or microfiche can be obtained by calling the NTIS sales desk at (703) 557-4650 to request order forms and pricing information and then by mailing the order forms and payment to:

> U.S. Department of Commerce
> National Technical Information Service
> 5285 Port Royal Road
> Springfield, VA 22161

The report (John, 1977) available from Project Share, a national clearinghouse for improving the management of human services, can be ordered directly from that clearinghouse by writing to:

> Project Share
> P.O. Box 2309
> Rockville, MD 20852

Finally, the three materials available from private and commercial publishers can be ordered directly from these publishers at the following addresses:

> Praeger Special Studies
> 200 Park Avenue
> New York, NY 10017

Greater Portland Work Education Council
710 S. W. Second Avenue
Portland, OR 97204

Langwood Division
Allyn and Bacon, Inc.
Link Drive
Rockleigh, NJ 07647

* * *

Delahanty, D., Frank, J., & Riisen, A. *Community readiness: Preparing for the coordination of human services.* Louisville, KY: Human Services Coordination Alliance, 1975. (National Technical Information Service No. SHR-0001643)

This is the first in a series of ten manuals on interagency coordination prepared by the Human Services Coordination Alliance, a locally funded project in Kentucky. Interagency cooperation is considered to be a sequential process made up of five stages: *awakening, exploring and specifying, sanctioning, demonstrating,* and *sustaining.* During the first stage, awakening, agency administrators become aware that there are conditions in the community for which past solutions are ineffective or inappropriate. The authors describe the kinds of conditions that would cause a community to consider interagency coordination seriously for the first time. The next section, exploring and specifying, covers the processes of identifying key people who need to be brought together (and whose functions need to be coordinated) and of defining the scope of activities to include in the coordination effort. This discussion complements Chapter 1 of our guide by suggesting that participants should be divided into policy and technical committees and by recommending how to use consultants on the project. Stage III is sanctioning—the critical period during which the interagency project becomes a formal and officially sanctioned organization with a formal work plan. The authors discuss how to hire project staff and whether to reimburse agencies that are donating staff. During the fourth stage, the potential of interagency activities is demonstrated by designing and developing the project's first product. The text on how to find funding for coordination can be read along with the section on finding resources for interagency coordination in this volume. Finally, the stage of sustaining covers expansion and evaluation of project activities. The discussion is general and does not explain how to evaluate a project, but the description of how project goals and activities should change after the first successful product is completed does provide a perspective on the evolution of a coordination project that is relevant to any evaluation attempt.

Gans, S. P., & Horton, G. T. *Integration of human services: The state and municipal levels.* New York: Praeger, 1975.

This book is one of the most comprehensive and detailed pieces of research on integration of services available. The data are drawn from case studies and evaluations of a selected sample of 30 integration projects across the country. Early chapters summarize the findings and recommendations of the study, Chapters 6 through 12 provide comparative analyses of the projects on a number of dimensions, and Chapter 13 contains case studies of the more instructive projects with their interesting features highlighted. Chapter 6 describes the range of factors facilitating and inhibiting integration of services, the frequency with which they occur, and the significance of their impact. The 52 facilitators and 36 inhibitors are categorized, and the categories are ranked according to the amount of their influence on the success or failure of the project. Then, within each category, the particular facilitating or inhibiting factors are analyzed separately. This chapter complements Chapter 2 of our guide. Because the projects were all funded by the Department of Health, Education, and Welfare and hired project staff, however, the effects of grant administration policies and the characteristics of project staff are stressed more than in this volume. Chapter 7 describes the range of integrating linkages that can be developed, the conditions under which they are most likely to be appropriate, and their significance for developing other integrative linkages among agencies. Gans and Horton differentiate between *direct service linkages* and *administrative linkages* and between *voluntary* coordination projects, *mediated* projects, and *directed* projects. The frequency of development of each linkage under various conditions is described, and their impacts on *accessibility, continuity,* and *efficiency* of client services are assessed. This chapter covers many of the same kinds of interagency activities as Chapters 3, 4, and 5 of the present book, but instead of describing how to develop the linkages, the text analyzes linkages through the eyes of a researcher and evaluator. Chapter 8 of Gans and Horton's book discusses various roles that clients can play in integration projects, and Chapters 9, 10, 11, and 12 describe directed, mediated, and voluntary projects and neighborhood service centers in more detail. Should you want to review detailed findings from research studies on interagency coordination, *Integration of Human Services* is one of the best places to start.

Hoover, B. *Handbook: How to set up a work education council.* Portland, OR: Greater Portland Work Education Council, 1980.

The purpose of this handbook is to provide a practical guide for communities that want to establish work education councils. A work education council is a special kind of coordination project that brings

BIBLIOGRAPHY

together education agencies, youth service agencies, local government, private employers, and labor organizations for the purpose of improving the school-to-work transition for youth in a community. However, even if your organization or agency is not involved in vocational training or employment, you will find many of the ideas in the handbook generalizable to your cooperative planning situation. Chapter 2, for example, contains discussions of how to identify goals and priorities for a project, how to secure funds, and reasons for hiring a project director rather than using a staff person loaned by a participating agency. Six suggestions are presented for operation of a coordinated project, covering membership, leadership, task forces (subcommittees responsible for particular activities), and setting up a meeting schedule. An especially interesting section of this chapter deals with conditions and problems commonly found in rural areas: overcommitted community leaders, lack of occupational diversity, longer transportation distances to meetings, and gaps in needed services, programs, and community statistics. Chapter 3 is devoted to potential problems and pitfalls, some of which are not specific to work education councils. One useful topic that is included (and is *not* dealt with explicitly in the present volume) is how to regain the interest of or replace inactive project members. Some of the strategies that are presented are worth considering along with the activities presented in Chapter 2 of our guide as ways of encouraging the active participation of agency administrators in interagency council activities.

John, D. *Managing the human service "system": What have we learned from services integration?* Washington, DC: Project Share, 1977. (Project Share, Human Services Monograph Series No. 4; DHEW Publication No. OS-76-130).

The twenty coordination projects reviewed in this report attempted a variety of interagency activities that augment the discussions of Chapters 2, 3, and 4 of our volume. One of the projects involved state- and local-level staff in efforts to support multicounty human service boards. Six projects planned and operated multiagency service centers, while three other projects developed multiagency client information systems and two others engaged exclusively in interagency planning activities. The remaining projects designed and implemented a wide variety of cooperative service arrangements. A categorization system of 29 specific types of interagency linkages classified into six major groups (*fiscal, personnel, planning and programming, administrative support, core services,* and *case coordination*) is used to describe and synthesize the activities, problems, and successes of the projects. To be sure, the projects met with many of the obstacles to coordination described in Chapter 2 of our guide. The suggestions for overcoming these obstacles provided by the most successful

projects reiterate the importance of persistence in the face of much
built-in adversity. From these projects, the author concludes that

1. building interagency linkages is a difficult process that demands
   great political skills and an incremental, or step-by-step, approach;
   and
2. interagency linkages can improve service delivery but are unlikely to
   cut costs.

With the first point we heartily agree. As to the second, remember that,
too often, new services are added at the same time coordination projects
are begun, with the usual (and expected) result being that *more cannot be
done for less.* For this reason, please keep in mind the benefits of
coordination presented in Chapter 1, especially the statement concerning
greater efficiency:

> Interagency coordination can help an agency to deliver *more services
> for the same money,* or the *same services for less money,* through
> economies of scale, reduction of duplication, and improved cost-
> benefit ratios.

Joint Center for Human Services Development. *Integration of services is a
process, not a product.* San Jose, CA: San Jose State University, School
of Social Work, 1976. (National Technical Information Service No.
SHR-0001174)

The title of this report is also its major finding—the integration of
human services is a *process,* not a program, product, or place. Through a
lengthy process of identifying obstacles to coordination and preparing for
interagency training workshops for local-level staff, the authors learned
that the problem-solving and interpersonal skills of the people involved in
coordination efforts are at least as important as the design of the interagency programs. For this reason, the workshops that were conducted
focused on the issues of resolving conflicts, clarifying roles, and communicating with others. The resource materials that were developed for these
workshops are appended to the report and will probably be of value to
readers of our guide (especially Chapter 5) who want to prepare their
co-workers for multiagency approaches to meeting community needs. Perhaps the best way our readers can decide whether these materials would be
of use is by reviewing selected staff-related obstacles to coordination the
authors of this report found to be most common and for which they
designed the workshops. If any of these conditions seems familiar, consider ordering the report.

Issues Affecting the Individual

1. Low morale (such as feelings of frustration, disappointment)
2. Lack of motivation to engage in services integration
3. Many unmet personal needs among service workers
4. Perception of threat to security by integration or reorganization
5. Loss of autonomy in collaborative arrangements
6. Uncertainty created by job changes
7. Threat of becoming anonymous in a complex system
8. Lack of individual flexibility to assume new roles
9. Feeling of powerlessness to affect an integrated system
10. Low or unrealistically high expectations for success
11. Personal values and principles that clash with organizational activities
12. Perceived threat of coordination to career lines and upward mobility

Lauffer, A. *Assessment tools: For practitioners, managers, planners and trainers.* Beverly Hills, CA: Sage Publications, 1982.

Lauffer points out that assessment can be used to examine what is, what is likely to be, and what ought to be. While each of the eight assessment tools he describes are applicable to interorganizational exchange and coordination, he uses these themes as the exemplars for those tools. Thus, in Chapter 2, he shows how *ecomapping* can be used to identify the range of current and potential linkages between social agencies at the community level. The glossary of terms and suggestions for focus complement the discussion in our book fully.

LINK, a simulation game in which participants are challenged to develop programmatically, politically, and fiscally sound exchanges, goes beyond mapmaking to exploration of the interactional tasks that are required for effective interagency coordination. Instructions for "play" are found in Chapter 7 on "the aim of the game." Participants include agency administrators and program personnel, community influentials, consumer groups and their representatives, funding agencies, and others. The game can be used to introduce participants to all of the potential exchanges possible in their communities or to test out the implications of one or another coordinating mechanism.

Lauffer also deals with interorganizational exchange from a community planning perspective in his volume, *Social Planning at the Community Level* (Englewood Cliffs, NJ: Prentice-Hall, 1978). In Chapters 6 and 7, he focuses explicitly on the role of the individual planner or organizer and his or her use of leverage in promoting coordination and exchange.

Neal, D. C., Bailey, W. J., & Ross, B. E. *Strategies for school improvement: Cooperative planning and organization development.* Boston: Allyn and Bacon, 1981.

As its preface states, "this is a book about how to improve elementary and secondary schools in a time when enrollments are declining, resources are scarce, and the public is pessimistic about school reform." Because the same lack of resources and public skepticism affect other human services agencies, the suggestions of how school administrators can work with other agencies in the community to maintain adequate service levels are also appropriate for the administrators of other service agencies. Chapters 5 and 16, for example, discuss the dynamics of meaningful collaboration and commonly encountered obstacles. These chapters provide useful and more theoretical supplements to the discussions in Chapter 2 of our guide. Chapter 17, which discusses administrative issues concerned with inter-agency partnerships, is also a useful addendum to Chapter 2 and, in describing the specific issues to be resolved by joint planning bodies, provides some ideas for proceeding with the administration of integrated programs (see our Chapter 5). Chapter 20, "Evaluation Tactics," and Appendix D, "How to Evaluate Education Programs," also amplify many of the points raised in Chapter 5 of our book. Finally, Appendix E, "Consortium Policies and Procedures," provides insights on the form and contents of interagency council charters (such as memoranda of agreement among agency directors, specifying their roles in interagency planning) that may be needed in forming a local planning council (see our Chapter 2) or in readying this group to fund and administer jointly an integrated services system (see our Chapter 5).

ABOUT THE AUTHORS

Robert J. Rossi, Kevin J. Gilmartin, and *Charles W. Dayton* are social scientists at the American Institutes for Research. Their master's and doctoral degrees range from English to cognitive psychology, from education to philosphy. Their research in recent years has focused on the development of innovative strategies for agencies to use in working together to meet the needs of their communities. For the past three years, they have assisted and monitored cooperative planning demonstration projects and have prepared this guide.

Jurgen Wolff, who illustrated this volume, is a communications specialist with the American Institutes for Research and also a freelance writer and artist. He claims that all of his illustrations are serious drawings done in the style of the old masters, but since he never paid attention during art classes they end up looking like cartoons.

Hoskins never wrote or read a line of text in this guide and, frankly, was counting entirely on seniority to avoid having to learn anything about interagency coordination. He has since been transferred to an extremely distant branch office.